Ellen Pifer

NABOKOV
and the
Novel

HARVARD UNIVERSITY PRESS
Cambridge, Massachusetts
and London, England
1980

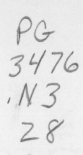

Copyright © 1980 by the President and Fellows of Harvard
College
All rights reserved
Printed in the United States of America

Publication of this book has been aided by a grant from the
Andrew W. Mellon Foundation

Library of Congress Cataloging in Publication Data

Pifer, Ellen.
    Nabokov and the novel.

    Includes bibliographical references and index.
    1.   Nabokov, Vladimir Vladimirovich, 1899-1977—
Criticism and interpretation.   I.   Title.
PG3476.N3Z8   813'.54   80-16197
ISBN 0-674-59840-7

Preface

No one disputes Vladimir Nabokov's brilliance as a
stylist. His language may startle, tease, disturb; but,
most readers agree, it rarely disappoints. Wit, craft,
elegance, originality—these words are most often
heard when a Nabokov novel is being discussed. Yet
a steady barrage of negative criticism has, for half a
century, accompanied the frequent praise. Many of
the same readers who laud Nabokov's genius for
language tend to regard his verbal pyrotechnics as
evidence of the aesthete's shallow psychology. The
primary responsibility of the novelist is, after all, to
depict human beings and their struggles in the world.
But Nabokov, we often hear it said, preferred patterns to people and the challenges of art to the
intractable problems of life.

My intention in this book is to demonstrate that
even the most intricate of Nabokov's artifices reflect
the author's abiding interest in human beings, not
only as artists and dreamers but as ethical beings sub-

ject to moral law and sanction. Because Nabokov's characters are frequently charged with being mere puppets of their master, my point of departure is, as the title of the first chapter indicates, "the question of character." What claim to reality have characters who exist in a world of declared artifice? The answer to that question presupposes the answer to another: What, in Nabokov's view, makes up human reality? My analysis of a representative body of his fiction is meant to provide some answers to these questions, along with conclusive evidence that Nabokov does, in fact, seek to reflect "reality" in his novels. The conclusions drawn in chapters 2 through 5 culminate in the formulation of still another question—the question of Nabokov's contribution to the tradition of the novel. In chapter 6, therefore, I invite the reader to take a speculative pause, posing in an informal rather than theoretical manner "the question of realism." In the final two chapters, I reexamine Nabokov's notorious quest for "aesthetic bliss" in the light of his less celebrated, but no less ardent, commitment to moral truth.

Rather than provide a comprehensive survey of all of Nabokov's fiction, I deliberately focus attention on those novels which are the most highly wrought and aesthetically self-conscious. If the reader is convinced by my discussion of the most "artificial" and detached fictions, I shall have made my case for Nabokov's achievement as a novelist. In selecting, from the impressive variety of Nabokov's complete works, those novels which come under special consideration here, I have also kept in mind the number, subject, and quality of previous critical studies. *Lolita* and

Pale Fire, for example, have already been the focus of much excellent and wide-ranging criticism. For this reason, I have chosen to examine these two established masterpieces of the Nabokov canon in relation to a less familiar work, the Russian novel *Despair*. Although *Lolita* and *Pale Fire* may appear to receive relatively brief attention, sandwiched as they are within the confines of a single chapter, I actually refer to them throughout the book. The celebrated humanity of these two novels is no artistic fluke, but the result of themes everywhere present in Nabokov's fiction. *King, Queen, Knave*, the subject of an early chapter, may be unfamiliar to some readers. The fact that this novel is usually dismissed as intricate but lifeless, because devoid of interesting lifelike characters, raised in my mind certain fundamental questions about the nature of Nabokov's fiction. While reading *King, Queen, Knave*, I began to examine the way in which Nabokov's detachment from his characters and their "invented habitus" contributes dramatically to a moral perception of reality.

My analysis of the novels originally written in Russian is based on Nabokov's most recent English versions. When reference to the original Russian text appears necessary, I supply the information in a note. This method best serves the majority of my readers, who, I assume, have read Nabokov in English. It also serves my argument, because in almost every case the revised English versions of earlier Russian works incorporate more elaborate patterns of artifice, creating a greater awareness of the author's manipulation of the fiction. It is my contention that Nabokov's increasingly sophisticated use of artifice is not developed at the expense of the novelist's commitment to creating character, as many critics tend to assume.

I am grateful to the University of Delaware for a General University Research Grant that enabled me to complete this book. Typing costs and other related expenses were also met by a University grant-in-aid, awarded by the College of Arts and Science. *Modern Fiction Studies* and *Slavic and East European Journal* kindly granted me permission to reprint chapters 7 and 8, which originally appeared, in slightly different form, in their pages. I wish to express my special thanks to Robert Alter, whose interest in this project was a continuing source of encouragement during its development. Simon Karlinsky, Robert Hughes, Eric Johannesson, and the late F. W. Dupee—all astute readers of Nabokov—encouraged me, at various times, in my study. Finally, I want to thank my husband, Drury Pifer, for his enthusiasm and support during this undertaking.

Contents

Contents

ALL NOVELISTS
are fundamentally seekers
and describers of the real,
but the realism of each novelist
will depend on his view
of the ultimate reaches
of reality.

FLANNERY O'CONNOR

CHAPTER I

The Question
of Character

"I have reached the original conclusion that if one performs at least one good act per day (even if it is nothing more than giving one's place to an elderly person on the tram) life becomes exceedingly more pleasant. In the final analysis everything in the world is very simple and founded upon two or three not very complicated truths."[1] Thus the young Vladimir Nabokov wrote to his mother in September 1924, at the age of twenty-five. Have we caught the young dandy napping, lapsing into virtue for the sake of a parent whom he adored? Or does this simple and (as the letter writer is quick to acknowledge) *un*original disclosure of human sympathy suggest how inaccurate may be the myths that have grown up around the celebrated novelist? In review after review, as well as in numerous critical books and scholarly articles, Nabokov is presented as an aesthete indifferent to the everyday struggles of humanity—an artist in perpetual flight from the sordid realities of this world, soar-

ing like Icarus into the realm of "aesthetic bliss."[2]
This perspective on Nabokov's literary achievement
is surprisingly widespread, and it has fostered some
grave misconceptions about his enterprise as a novelist.

My intention is to correct some of these misconceptions and to compensate for certain perplexing omis-
sions, call them gaps in analysis, which I detect in the
considerable body of criticism thus far devoted to
Nabokov's fiction. This is not to suggest that a great
deal of perceptive critical work does not already exist,
but only to demonstrate that while Nabokov's repu-
tation as a master stylist remains uncontested, some
essential matters concerning his fiction's *content* have
been overlooked or dismissed. Such an arbitrary distinction between form and content is, I admit, a
rather clumsy and certainly outmoded critical approach. Yet I call attention to it here because this is
the premise on which rests so much of the hostile criticism directed at Nabokov's work. His verbal pyrotechnics are frequently singled out as evidence of the
master's obsession with aesthetic form and his disdain
for the novelist's traditional concerns, which have
always been allied with the struggles of imperfect humanity. Nabokov's prose may be dazzling, we often
hear it said, but such magic is achieved at the expense
of his human material—those unfortunate characters
of his, so flattened by the constrictions of formal design. Nabokov apparently preferred "cards and chess-
men," puppets and paper figures, to convincingly real
characters; for puppets are less likely to unsettle elegant patterns with disturbing signs of vitality.[3] Art
triumphs, but at the expense of life, and the cost is

2

accounted for in numerous critical evaluations of Nabokov's literary production. No matter how admirable their form, his artifices are, in the last analysis, assessed as inferior works of novelistic creation. In the opinion of many critics, they lack the requisite moral and psychological profundity that qualifies select works of fiction to take their place in the novel's great tradition.

Those who champion Nabokov's fiction, on the other hand, tend to argue that the creation of character is simply not of central importance to his work. The heart of these novels lies elsewhere—in an examination of the artistic process itself. Andrew Field, for example, finds that if the critic approaches every Nabokov novel as an elucidation of the means by which art is created, he will have discovered "a universal key which 'works' [to explain] almost all of Nabokov's fiction."[4] Making extensive use of this "key" throughout his own study of Nabokov's Russian and English works, Field concludes that the murder that takes place in Nabokov's Russian novel *Despair* is a strange "allegory of the artistic process," as is the "lust and child-molestation" in *Lolita*. The latter is "a tale representing the tragic pain and entrancing beauty of art and the tremendous price it exacts."[5] Now the danger of approaching every Nabokov novel as an exposition of the problems of art lies in the potential reduction of the novel's specific and troubling psychic impact to the safer (and more remote) plane of general ideas. In this way, we note, mad Hermann's murder of Felix in *Despair* and Humbert's "lust and child-molestation" are reduced by Field to mere symbolic events representing the far more palatable process of artistic discovery. As Nabokov himself once put it, "the discovered wild fruit" of the text is thus boiled down to "synthetic jam."[6] As a defense of the values of Nabokov's art, such metaphoric explanations do not hold up very well, either. What a receptive critic interprets as an illuminating exposition of the process of artistic creation is quite easily dismissed by the unreceptive critic as an aesthete's trivial display of self-love.

The difficulty of assessing Nabokov's achievement as a novelist writing about people obviously derives from the flagrantly artificial quality of his fiction. Current sophisticated theories of criticism notwithstanding, readers of novels have traditionally tended to identify the *artificial* with the *superficial*. The Nabokovian universe, we all know, is a construct of words, taking life from the page and pen of its author. Self-conscious artifice intrudes on the reader's awareness, signaling the discontinuities between Nabokov's fabricated worlds and the one we call our own. According to Nabokov himself, upon completing one of his novels the reader should experience "a sensation of its world receding in the distance and stopping somewhere there suspended afar like a picture in a picture."[7] It is not only at the end of his novels, however, that Nabokov arranges his effects in this way. The continuous word-play, allusions, self-conscious references, and authorial intrusions all serve to interrupt the reader's sympathetic participation in the author's illusory world. In this way, Nabokov alerts us to the fictional status of his literary landscape; he impels us to recognize that all the apparent depth and dimension we perceive in this "picture in a picture" are achieved aesthetic effects.

In traditional novels, on the other hand, the effects of depth—psychological as well as physical—derive from the apparent solidity of the three-dimensional reality being evoked. Here the operations of the artist are covert, the novelist employing all the strategies of literary perspective (a different kind of artifice) to lead our attention away from the flat surface of the page. Characters in a traditional novel are, in accord with the author's striving for a sense of general reality, presented as autonomous beings freely moving in three-dimensional space. The apparent autonomy of their literary existence, quite naturally, plays an important part in making them convincing representations of human beings.[8] Nabokov's characters, by contrast, are overtly manipulated by an author who behaves like a despot. Deprived of lifelike autonomy, subject to the strictures of artifice, can such creatures, we ask, claim any depth and dimension—any real life —of their own? The answer is, I believe, a resounding yes, but to arrive at this affirmation we must consider, first of all, the deeper implications of Nabokov's notorious fascination with the powers of language.

The most familiar assumption is that Nabokov's "lush verbal jungle" (as one distinguished critic recently wrote) is an obvious manifestation of the decadent writer, whose excessive preoccupation with language stems from an exhaustion with life. Yet while numerous critics have, over half a century, assumed that Nabokov's delight in language evinces a preference for art over life, he himself regarded the process of verbal creation as, above all, *life-giving*. In a long passage in *Bend Sinister*, Nabokov calls his reader's attention to the intimate relationship that exists between language and life. The passage occurs as the philosopher, Adam Krug, considers the mysterious process by which Shakespeare brought his characters to life in words: "Nature had once produced an Englishman whose domed head had been a hive of words; a man who had only to breathe on any particle of his stupendous vocabulary to have that particle live and expand and throw out tremulous tentacles until it became a complex image with a pulsing brain and correlated limbs."[9] Nature created Shakespeare who, in turn, inspired life in the creatures of his imagination through language—fusing words into live entities as magically as Nature sparks life in a combination of cells. Why, we might ask, did Nabokov emphasize this miraculous creation of life if, as so many assume, he was indifferent to creating live characters? In the foregoing passage he dramatizes the sense of irrepressible vitality involved in the creation of a character: Shakespeare's head is a teeming "hive" of words; he "breathes" on these inanimate particles, makes them "live and expand and throw out tremulous tentacles" until they develop a brain "pulsing" with its own vital processes. Contrary to the aestheticism we are told to expect from Nabokov, the emphasis here is not on the more exotic delights of word formation but on the absolute *vitality* of literary creation. The same emphasis occurs in a passage from Nabokov's autobiography, *Speak, Memory*. Here he describes the novelist as "building a *live* world from the most unlikely ingredients—rocks, and carbon, and blind throbbings."[10] Like a "deity," the artist breathes life into inanimate elements, the rocks and carbon of inert language, to create a living universe of fiction.

The quoted passage from *Bend Sinister* describes the birth of a literary character; yet despite the vital signs of life, this character significantly retains his literary identity as a "complex image," not a natural being. We recognize that literary creation is analogous to, rather than identical with, natural creation. Shakespeare, a mortal, obviously did not create other mortals. Only Nature, or God, may do that. Shakespeare's genius lay in forging the particles of language into vital human images, metaphors embodying the distinct qualities of human life within a verbal matrix. The laws of this kind of creation are aesthetic, not physical; the medium is language, and the creative force is individual human consciousness. Authors are deities, or despots, only in a limited sense. They create not Frankenstein's monster but literary characters, as Mary Shelley did. These are simple enough distinctions. Nevertheless, in our discussions of novels we frequently forget simple truths and assume that characters who remind us of their dependence on their creator cannot be taken seriously. We may be as outraged to recognize that a character has no autonomy within a work of fiction as if it were suggested that we ourselves had none. We feel insulted, disillusioned, or even attacked.

Such a confusion of simple truths may derive from the very nature of the novel—its singular capacity to incorporate the substance and rhythms of daily life

7

within its extended form. The behavior of novelistic characters may so closely resemble that of real people that we, as readers, tend to forget how thoroughly the fate of these characters has been dictated by an omnipotent author. And when an author like Nabokov draws attention to his godly manipulations, we tend to assume that he is depriving his characters, and us, of some essential freedom that is granted to mankind by other, more "humane" novelists. Thus we find many distinguished critics who, like Hugh Kenner, object to Nabokov's pervasive control of his characters' fate while overlooking the fact that all novelists, no matter how covert their manipulations, are just as guilty of the charge: "As a narrator who fuses with V.[,] Nabokov effects the destiny of Pnin, so what *happens* in these big and little worlds is what V. Nabokov has decreed shall happen, right down to the passage of an 'inquisitive butterfly' across a tennis court in 'Champion, Colorado,' between Humbert Humbert and Dolores Haze, in a paragraph all to itself."[11]

Instead of provoking indignation, our reading of Nabokov's fiction should encourage us to clarify some familiar distinctions. The freedom of a literary character is always illusory. A realist may attempt to make what "happens" to his character appear to rise inevitably out of his nature or the nature of the world posited by the fiction, but the form of a character's fate is always the author's choice. Plausibility is both natural and artificial; and while Nabokov's worlds declare themselves fiction, their author recognized the need for plausibility and consistency within their structure. He made this very clear when he described the social "inconsistencies" in Pushkin's treatment of his socially defined hero, Eugene Onegin: "I remain with Pushkin in Pushkin's world . . . I am concerned only with Pushkin's overlooking . . . that Onegin, who according to Pushkin is a punctilious *homme du monde* and an experienced duelist, would hardly choose a servant for a second or shoot to kill in the kind of humdrum affair where vanity is amply satisfied by sustaining one's adversary's fire without returning it."[12] An author must remain true to whatever observable social or physical facts he introduces into his fictional matrix. Nabokov based his own reading of Joyce's *Ulysses*, therefore, on those very realities of man's physiological condition to which Joyce devoted so much attention in the novel: "One of the reasons Bloom cannot be the active party in the Nighttown chapter . . . is that Bloom, a wilting male anyway, has been drained of his manhood earlier in the evening and thus would be quite unlikely to indulge in the violent sexual fancies of Nighttown."[13]

With regard to his own work, Nabokov appears to have disagreed with the allegorical mode of interpretation favored by Field and others. He described the shift in narrative tone at the end of *Lolita* not as a way to illuminate the process of art but as a means to "convey a constriction of the narrator's sick heart, a warning spasm causing him to abridge names and hasten to conclude his tale before it was too late."[14] Dismissing a metaphoric interpretation of the novel, Nabokov regarded this stylistic effect as an illumination of Humbert's specific character, not of the artist's general problems. One may argue whether or not the device in this case succeeds; this question involves a critical judgment on the reader's part. The author's intent, however, is quite clear—to reflect a change in the character's verbally rendered *psychological* state.

There are constants in human life that affect literary plausibility, like the sexual limitations of adult males alluded to in Nabokov's statement about *Ulysses*. There are also historical and social realities, as he indicated in his comments on Pushkin. We know that while writing *Lolita*, Nabokov took "a protracted series of local bus rides" to note the peculiarities of contemporary American teen-age jargon.[15] Despite these facts, plausibility is, for the most part, a relative matter. A character who is plausible in Pushkin's world is hardly going to be plausible in Flaubert's, and certainly not in Gogol's. (This contention would hold true even if all three had written in the same place, at the same time, and in the same language.) Plausibility of character is connected to the author's vision of reality and to the logic of his method in rendering this reality. Thus Nabokov prefaced his comments by saying, "I remain with Pushkin in Pushkin's world." The inconsistency he noted in *Eugene Onegin* is not based on a contradiction between Pushkin's view of humanity and Nabokov's own, but on a contradiction within the terms of the world of *Eugene Onegin* itself. Whether a realist or a declared artificer, the good novelist seeks to make his characters consistently conform to the logic of the world he depicts. In this sense, Balzac's or Zola's creatures are no more autonomous than Nabokov's; they are ruled by their authors' literary versions of universal laws. Outside the realm of the fiction, these laws are subject to debate. They are not objectively true, but subjectively convincing.

What I am suggesting, then, is that we may be denying Nabokov's characters their reality because of a misreading of, or disenchantment with, his method. The lives of literary characters (and, indeed, our own lives) are a great deal less autonomous than we would often like to believe. What we may resent, when reading a Nabokov novel, is the loss of our illusions rather than any inherent lack of humanity on the author's part. Shattering such illusions was a feat Nabokov particularly enjoyed. Obviously anticipating the stir his pronouncement would create, he once told an interviewer, "My characters are galley slaves."[16] The description is characteristically inciting; yet it contains more honesty than arrogance. Nabokov's love of puns is surely evident here in his use of the word "galley," which refers to the printer's proofs of a manuscript as well as to an ancient rowing vessel. Nabokov's characters serve their literary master; but slaves, after all, are puppets only in the social sense. Their lack of autonomy does not necessarily rob them of intrinsically human qualities. All literary characters are, quite frankly, pressed into service by a master whose ambitions they serve. Individual and collective experience is metamorphosed by each author into images of the human condition as he perceives it. An author's creatures depend on him for their life and the values inherent in it. All literary versions of human beings, whether fictional or actual historical figures, serve the author who creates, or re-creates, them. The act of writing about real people in one's memoirs or diary was thus described by Nabokov as the process by which "living persons" become "the performing poodles of the diarist's act."[17] Characters live or die within the language of their creator; they are, in a sense, his human figures of speech. The absolute responsibility of an author for his characters was, for Nabokov, a point of artistic honor and a sign of literary acumen. Asked if a character had ever, according to E. M. Forster's well-known description, taken hold of him or dictated the course of a novel's action, Nabokov replied: "I have never experienced this. What a preposterous experience! Writers who have had it must be very minor or insane. No, the design of my novel is fixed in my imagination and every character follows the course I imagine for him. I am the perfect dictator in that private world insofar as I alone am responsible for its stability and truth."[18]

Insisting on the unique logic, stability, and truth of a particular work of fiction, Nabokov deplored the "old-fashioned, naïve, and musty method of human-interest criticism . . . that consists of removing the characters from an author's imaginary world to the imaginary, but generally far less plausible, world of the critic who then proceeds to examine these displaced characters as if they were 'real people.' "[19] The discomfort we sometimes experience with Nabokov may well stem from our inability to remove *his* characters from the world of artifice and settle them neatly within the context of our own. The intrusive patterns of his authorial design do not provide a reassuring sense of interchange between his world and ours. Yet, as I have said, this apparent loss of direct contact with, or participation in, the author's world is largely illusory. The relationship of a work of fiction to the world of immediate experience is always a figurative one, in much the same way that a model of the atom or of the universe is only a structural analogy. Such models, and the various data of our experience which they help us to organize, are as close as we ever come to grasping the essence of reality. It is always by means of such constructs, or artifice, that we represent the world to ourselves. Why should we assume, then, that Nabokov's presentation of reality through artifice is any less serious an epistemological enterprise? Art is, for Nabokov, a means of grappling with the nature of reality, not a retreat from it. It is on this assumption, so frequently overlooked in Nabokov's case, that I want to base my analysis of a representative body of his work, seeking to clarify at each point the psychological, moral, and metaphysical issues his fiction raises. By thus confronting what, in Nabokov's view, actually makes up human reality, we may discover the basis on which he, as a novelist, claims "real life" for the characters who exist in his "private world" of art.

CHAPTER II

Consciousness, Real Life, and Fairytale Freedom: *King, Queen, Knave*

In the foreword to the 1968 English translation of *King, Queen, Knave*, first published in Russian in 1928, Nabokov wrote: "Of all my novels this bright brute is the gayest. Expatriation, destitution, nostalgia had no effect on its elaborate and rapturous composition." At this time, Nabokov said, he was dissatisfied with the " 'human humidity,' *chelovecheskaya vlazhnost'*, permeating [his] first novel *Mashen'ka*," published in 1926. If novels, as E. M. Forster remarked, are "sogged with humanity," then Nabokov apparently set out to cure his second novel of this chronic condition. For *King, Queen, Knave* he chose "a set of exclusively German characters," although he claimed he "spoke no German, had no German friends, had not read a single German novel either in the original, or in translation." In art as well as nature, Nabokov pointed out, such "a glaring disadvantage may turn out to be a subtle protective device."[1] From what dangers, we may ask, did the

14

young writer find it necessary to protect his fiction? Ought we to assume, like those who regard Nabokov as exclusively an aesthete, that the emotional detachment sought in *King, Queen, Knave* is an early sign of his indifference to human psychology or "reality" as a subject for art?

The term "human humidity" suggests the novel's extraordinary capacity for creating sentimental effects, for moving its readers to tears. We are frequently "carried away" by novels, which draw us, unconscious and uncritical, into the web of their expansive worlds. The reader experiences an immediate and unchallenged identification with the fictional characters, entangled in the familiar conflicts and circumstances of daily life. Existence may be ultimately mysterious to us, but the daily, concrete living out of our existence becomes so familiar in its repetition that it ends by appearing inevitable and even predictable most of the time. The novel, containing more of life in its everyday, repetitive aspect than any other literary form, has the same power to present itself as something familiar and natural. For this reason, I believe, Nabokov saw a connection between the excessive "humidity" of his first novel and its quotidian familiarity: "The émigré characters I had collected in that display box [*Mashen'ka*] were so transparent to the eye of the era that one could easily make out the labels behind them" (foreword, p. viii). The novel's "human humidity" and the reader's uncritical identification with literary characters both thrive on the generally accepted ideas that circulate among people living in a particular historical era. To those buffeted by the tremendous social and political storms of the early

twentieth century, and especially to the Russian émigré population scattered throughout Europe, the influence of history on the individual's immediate life
threatened to be overwhelming. By creating characters with whom he had, "ethnopsychically," nothing
in common, Nabokov elected to distance himself in
King, Queen, Knave from the émigré's natural preoccupation with social reality. Here it is important to
understand that a lack of social identification with his
characters does not necessarily signal Nabokov's
shrinking interest in human psychology. His impatience with social "labels" reveals, on the contrary, a
desire to create character in a new way. Nabokov's
break was not with humanity or the human predicament but with the novelist's traditional regard for historical process as the modern form of fate.

Political revolutions, technological innovations,
and social conditions have been grist for generations
of novelists. As Mary McCarthy has said, novels are
obliged to "carry the news." She adds: "We do really
(I think) expect a novel to be true, not only true to
itself, like a poem, or a statue, but true to actual life
. . . We not only make believe we believe a novel, but
we do substantially believe it, as being continuous
with real life . . . and the presence of fact in fiction, of
dates and times and distances, is a kind of reassur-
ance—a guarantee of credibility."[2] Denying such
guarantees from the outset, Nabokov said of his second novel, "I might have staged *KQKn* in Rumania or
Holland [instead of Berlin]" (foreword, p. viii). With
studied detachment he rejects the diligent pursuit of
"credibility" engaged in by novelists from Cervantes
to Tolstoy. Challenging "the accepted notion of a

'modern world' continuously flowing around us,"
Nabokov found such historical postulations to belong "to the same type of abstraction as say, the 'qua-
ternary period' of paleontology." In opposition to
these abstract historical classifications he posited the
more penetrating reality of specific imagination:
"What I feel to be the real modern world is the world
the artist creates . . . by the very act of his shedding,
as it were, the age he lives in."[3]

Nabokov's account of the artist "shedding" the age
he lives in, like a reptile emerging from a dead skin,
calls for no withdrawal from the world but a renewed
confrontation with it. The artist conceives reality
afresh only after he has deliberately separated himself
from the apparent world formulated every day by
those who direct the current interests and affairs of
society. A novelist who aims, in Mary McCarthy's
words, to "carry the news" of this world winds up
dragging the carapace of social-historical formulation
along with him. In *King, Queen, Knave*, on the other
hand, Nabokov deliberately estranged himself from
the generalizing influences and historical postulations
of his era. His discovery of the "fairytale freedom"
inherent in treating "an unknown milieu" led to his
"gradual inner disentanglement" from the immediate
pressures and assumptions of émigré life and, as a
consequence, from the novelist's inherited obligations
to social reality (foreword, p. viii). By disowning the
pursuit of literal "credibility," regarded as essential
by generations of novelists, Nabokov was able, moreover, to challenge those preconceptions of reality
which, consciously or not, most novelists disseminate
with the very "news" they seek to carry. Turning our

attention to *King, Queen, Knave*, the first of Nabokov's flagrantly artificial worlds, we shall begin to
examine the terms of this challenge.

Nabokov's declared detachment from his characters in *King, Queen, Knave* signals, as I have suggested, a break with formal tradition. Critics, noting
this detachment and taking into account the novel's
title, have found its characters to be mere "cardboard
figures."[4] Such labels only serve to obscure the pro-
vocative nature of Nabokov's methods of character
depiction in this novel. Franz, for example, the young
knave, is far too intensely rendered a character to be
dismissed, at the outset, as a paper figure. He becomes, in Nabokov's hands, a most ironic representative of *l'homme moyen sensuel*—that recurrent subject and special pride of the nineteenth-century novelist.[5] The stereotypical notion of the average man,
whose existence we regard as primarily *sensuel* and
carnal rather than psychic or spiritual, is exploded by
Nabokov's radical depiction of "physical Franz." Existence for Franz, it is true, consists almost entirely of
physical sensations, but those sensations crowd into a
void where refining and synthesizing human consciousness ought vigorously to operate. Franz is per-
petually afraid of existence because his perception is
clogged with indiscriminate sensory data that
threaten, at any time, to overwhelm his psyche and
set up a tyranny of hateful impressions. Any new,
unsavory impression impinging on Franz's cowardly
consciousness may unlock a psychic "chamber of
horrors," may flood his mind with disgusting images
of random physical life. Involuntarily, and much to
his horror, Franz may vividly recall a dog he has seen

vomiting, a child sucking on "a filthy thing resembling a baby's pacifier," or an old man in a streetcar firing "a clot of mucus into the ticket collector's hand" (pp. 3-4). When such images well up in Franz's victimized psyche, he is overcome by nausea. In Franz's case, predominantly carnal existence is shown to be neither normal nor average. "Physical Franz" is psychically ill.

Franz's moments of well-being also originate in physical sensation: "Warm, warmly flowing happiness filled physical Franz to the brim, pulsated in wrist and temple, pounded in his breast, and issued from his finger in a ruby drop when he pricked himself accidentally at the store" (p. 104). In this description, Nabokov cleverly subverts, while making use of, a familiar cliché. Human happiness is described as "brimming over" or "filling" the one who is happy. Based on a worn metaphor, the cliché locates the ephemeral state of happiness in the physical sensations that mental joy triggers in the body. Thus happiness is identified as physically warm and expansive, like the play of an excited pulse and mounting blood pressure. But Franz's experience of happiness is, quite literally, exposed as sheer physical sensation. Happiness *is* the "warmly flowing" blood that courses through his body, concretely issuing in a bright red drop.

In similar fashion, Franz's memory and imagination prove to be mere instruments of involuntary, quite painful sensation. "His recollections of school seemed always to be dodging away from possible, impossible, contacts with the grubby, pimply, slippery skin of some companion or other pressing him

19

to join in a game or eager to impart some spitterish secret" (p. 4). Franz's memory "dodges" from contact with memories that oppress him like bodies. For him even a secret, that exclusively human form of intimate communication, is a "spitterish" physical thing.

A more violent assault on Franz's senses takes place at the opening of the novel. He is comfortably seated in the third-class compartment of a moving train when a man with a disfigured face suddenly enters from the corridor. As soon as Franz sees the passenger's face, he is overcome by dread and nausea. The stranger's abnormal features reduce "physical Franz" to a state of sickening fear: "Most of the nose had gone or had never grown. To what remained of its bridge the pale parchment-like skin adhered with a sickening tightness; the nostrils had lost all sense of decency and faced the flinching spectator like two sudden holes, black and asymmetrical" (p. 3). The flawed face is a terrible apparition of the confounding physical reality that tyrannizes Franz. Those "black" and "sudden holes"—in place of ordinary features— suggest the black unknown yawning beneath the apparently arbitrary flux of physical phenomena. A flaw in the fabric of reality, the freakish face opens a chink through which Franz glimpses something terrifying. Characteristically, his fear takes the form of acute and painful physical sensation: "His tongue felt repulsively alive; his palate nastily moist. His memory opened its gallery of waxworks, and . . . at its far end somewhere a chamber of horrors awaited him" (p. 3). The gross ironies and accidents of carnal existence—like the old man spitting mucus into the conductor's hand and the child innocently sucking on what appears to be a discarded prophylactic—fill Franz with insane horror. In terms of our creatural existence, all human beings are ultimately as helpless as the old man and the unwitting child. We are easily made the fools of life's little jokes. Franz, a virtual prisoner of wayward physical life, is in this sense as in others the fool, or knave, of the novel.

While Franz shudders in repulsion at the hateful apparition of this monstrous face, the other passengers in the compartment are singularly unaffected: "And worst of all, the old ladies ignoring their foul neighbor [the noseless man] munched their sandwiches and sucked on fuzzy sections of orange" (p. 4). Repulsed even by the texture of the fruit, Franz propels himself into the second-class compartment of a wealthy businessman and his attractive wife. Dreyer, the businessman (who turns out, by Nabokov's design, to be Franz's uncle), eventually leaves the car in search of a newspaper; returning, he passes by the man with the deformed nose whose face has terrified Franz: "Glancing at him as he passed, Dreyer saw the grinning face of a grown man with the nose of a baby monkey. 'Curious,' thought Dreyer, 'ought to get such a dummy to display something funny' " (p. 16). Where Franz perceives a foul and terrifying monster, Dreyer sees just a funny nose. Both Franz and Dreyer encounter the passenger within the same temporal and spatial dimensions; yet the contrasting effects his deformity has on these two characters makes the stranger an oddly relative phenomenon. He terrifies no one but Franz; in fact, the other passengers hardly notice him. Dreyer, on the other hand, is amused by the freakish nose and promptly considers the possibil-

21

ities such a funny face has as a display model in his department store. One man's torture is another man's toy, and the reader is left with the job of assessing the problematical "objective" reality of this monster-clown, so dramatically metamorphosed by the contrary perceptions of Franz and his uncle Dreyer.

Many of Nabokov's critics, I am sure, would regard the noseless man's appearance in the novel as compromised, an obvious manifestation of the author's preference for manipulated artifice rather than convincing characterization. Disdaining the novelist's traditional regard for causal laws and verisimilitude, the author arbitrarily introduces the noseless passenger into the text. He merely contrives a handy coincidence so that Franz may join the Dreyers in their second-class compartment and get on with the plot. Nabokov, however, would have us assess the significance of his literary arrangements according to different criteria. Like everything else in his fiction, Nabokov's characters are overt creations of their author. Born of his perception, figured forth in words, assigned their own characteristic perceptions—their status is literary in a radical sense. They live not as reflections of a social-historical era but as representatives of human consciousness and its laws. For Nabokov, our "being aware of being aware of being" defines the essence of human existence and distinguishes man's life from the beast's.[6] The universe we inhabit is not an objectively measured Cartesian machine but a "universe embraced by consciousness."[7] In Nabokov's view, consciousness—and not the dynamics of planetary bodies or historical evolution—"is the only real thing in the world and the greatest mystery of all."[8]

Because language is the primary medium of consciousness, literature is in a special position to explore the nature of conscious life. In literature all representations of matter are distillations of perception; the only reality is that which has been created through acts of imaginative invention. Exploiting this fact of literary life, Nabokov examines the process by which individual consciousness creates the character of the perceived world. This is, of course, a radical inversion of the methods of formal realism, whereby fiction seeks authenticity by approximating our general notions of reality; such fiction may not deviate too far from what we recognize as familiar and plausible. In Nabokov's world, on the other hand, Franz, Dreyer, and the reader may all agree that the noseless man's face is deformed—lacking the ordinary configuration of bridge and nostrils. Beyond this, however, Nabokov does not labor to convince us of the probable appearance of the noseless man in an objective universe; rather, he is interested in the specific life that flows from the operation of uniquely delineated perception. Authenticity does not derive from Nabokov's convincing us of the probable existence of such noseless freaks, although he might have arranged things in this way. (Trains and buses are likely places for a novelist's characters to encounter the bizarre flotsam and jetsam of humanity.) In *King, Queen, Knave*, the noseless man's appearance is rendered incongruous, not natural. Rather than offer an explanation for his appearance in the novel, Nabokov heightens our awareness of the artifice, intentionally undermining the realistic illusion of causality and normalcy. The author shows his hand, but what it holds remains a mystery. He focuses his art at the point where general explanations for reality dissolve. Reality presents itself at the point where Franz's and Dreyer's perceptions diverge, not where they converge. If consciousness is "the only real thing in the world," then the novelist's obligations to reality are going to be radically defined. Nabokov strives to demonstrate how each of his characters particularizes and in a sense "makes strange" the general, familiar world men agree on for the sake of ontological comfort or social expediency. The "only real, authentic worlds," he once said, are "those that seem unusual."[9] Reality is not what appears so inevitable and familiar that we may easily identify with a literary character and his perceptions.

In a well-known essay, "Art as Device" ("Iskusstvo, kak priem"), Viktor Shklovsky, the Russian Formalist critic, examines the "general laws of perception," finding that "as one's actions grow habitual, they become automatic." To illustrate this process, Shklovsky cites the following passage from Tolstoy's diary:

> I was dusting a room and, walking around, approached the divan and couldn't remember whether or not I had dusted it. Since these movements are habitual and unconscious, I could not remember and felt that it was already impossible to remember; so that, if I had dusted and forgotten—that is, had acted unconsciously, then it was the same as if I had not. If someone conscious had been looking on, then the fact could be established. If, however, no one was

looking, or was looking on unconsciously, if the whole complex life of many people proceeds unconsciously, then it is as though this life had never been.

Commenting on Tolstoy's observations, Shklovsky remarks: "What is called art exists to restore the sensation of life, to make one feel things, to make the stone stony. The purpose of art is to impart the sensation of things as a form of perception rather than knowledge. The device of art is to make things 'strange,' to make form difficult—which increases the difficulty and duration of perception, since in art the process of perceiving is an end in itself and should be prolonged."[10]

The "difficult" nature of Nabokov's highly wrought artifices, the demands they make on the reader's perceptions, obviously fulfill Shklovsky's requirements for art. Less obvious, perhaps, is the fact that Nabokov, like Tolstoy, regarded the vital "process of perceiving" as fundamental to *life* as well as art. What Shklovsky identifies as the process of *ostranenie*, commonly translated "defamiliarization," operates within Nabokov's fiction as a psychological and epistemological principle. Artifice, rather than oppose life, is deployed by Nabokov to renew the reader's perception of reality—by estranging that perception from habitual formulations. As the act of perception becomes, in Nabokov's fiction, the focal point for examining reality, the general world, whose existence we automatically assume, tends to fade into the relatively unreal. From this vantage point, we can see how misleading it is to exempt Nabokov's characters from reality because they are deprived of apparent autonomy or of a seemingly objective social environment. The specific life or reality of Nabokov's characters depends, first and foremost, on the peculiar nature and quality of their rendered perceptions.

As I have already noted in the case of Franz and his uncle Dreyer, the characters of *King, Queen, Knave* have widely divergent perceptions and responses to their environment. Further events in the novel are, like the noseless man's appearance on the train, arranged by Nabokov to demonstrate the primary role of human consciousness in shaping reality. At one point, for example, Dreyer, his wife, Martha, and Franz, now Martha's clandestine lover, all attend a variety show together. Japanese trapeze artists, a juggler, and a performing seal regale the audience; then, after the intermission, a female violinist dressed "in silver shoes and a spangled evening dress" plays on a "luminous" violin with a "star-flashing bow." For the duration of the song, the violinist, her clothes, and the enlisted musical instrument are flooded by the alternating pink and green of busy spotlights. Martha and Franz quickly lose themselves in a swoon of sentimental music and sexual longing, but Dreyer abruptly interrupts them with a disgusted exclamation:

> [The violinist's] playing was languorous and really delicious and suffused Martha with such excitement, such exquisite sadness that she half-closed her eyes and found Franz's hand in the darkness; and he experienced the same sensation—a poignant rapture in harmony with their love. The musical phantasmagoria (as that item was listed) sparkled and swooned, the violin sang and moaned, the pink and green were joined by blue and violet—and then Dreyer could stand it no longer.
> "I have my eyes and ears closed," he said in a

26

weepy whisper, "let me know when this obscene abomination is over." (P. 117)

For a startled moment the swooning lovers fear they have been discovered—only to realize that the "obscene abomination" offending Dreyer's sensibilities is not their adulterous performance (to which he remains blind) but the trashy one occurring on stage. The amplification of banal effects by the changing floodlights betrays a form of degraded consciousness, employing technical means to simulate the magic of imagination.[11] For Dreyer, the violinist's performance is a travesty of human sensibility. Like all sham art, the light show lulls or deadens consciousness with its effects. Appetite and instinct may be aroused in this way, but never imagination. Disgusted as he is, Dreyer does not recognize the full implications of the violinist's banal performance. He does not sense the adulterers' "poignant rapture" nor the lust whetted in them by the sickly music.

The concluding entertainment at the variety show is a movie, in which agile chimpanzees ludicrously mimic human behavior: "On the flickering screen . . . a chimpanzee in degrading human clothes performed human actions degrading to an animal. Martha laughed heartily, remarking: 'Just look how smart he is!' Franz clucked his tongue in amazement, and insisted in all seriousness that it was a dwarf in disguise" (p. 118). As Nabokov's language here indicates, both man and beast are degraded by the circus imitation of one by the other. The mechanical reproduction of human gestures and activity does not begin to approximate the essential quality of human existence. That essence resides in consciousness, which cannot be simulated by beast or machine. Taking delight in this bumbling parody, Martha and Franz reveal themselves to be dangerously complacent about their own humanity. Franz's knavish contention that the bicycling chimp must be a dwarf in disguise bespeaks his own meager conception of the human.[12]

Degraded sensibility like Franz's is unable to assign proper priority to human consciousness. Franz's terror of existence partly arises from his having relinquished consciousness as a source of order, knowledge, and transcendence in the world. Franz lives in dread of the "chamber of horrors" that threatens to release, at any moment, a flood of involuntary images in his captive mind. By contrast, the creative exercise of consciousness signals a triumph of human imagination over the forces of darkness: "The bright mental image . . . conjured up by a wing-stroke of the will; *that* is one of the bravest movements a human spirit can make," avows Nabokov in *Speak, Memory*.[13] Franz's passive submission to Martha's domineering will, even when she devises a scheme to murder his uncle, is simply another aspect of his cowardly perception. True consciousness is a gift realized by its operation—not by mere possession; lacking exercise, the faculty atrophies. In Nabokov's view, human beings may forfeit their humanity out of torpor, sloth, or lack of will. As he once said, "Brains must work the hard way or else lose their calling and rank."[14]

What Nabokov seeks to depict, above all, is the process by which a character's consciousness establishes its own "rank" as an image of psychic existence.

An example of Nabokov's techniques for accomplishing this occurs in a passage describing Martha's adultery with Franz. Alluding to his literary predecessors, Flaubert and Tolstoy, who also wrote about adulteresses, the narrator points out that Martha is "no Emma and no Anna. In the course of her conjugal life she had grown accustomed to grant her favors to her wealthy protector [Dreyer, her husband] with such skill, with such calculation, with such efficient habits of physical practice, that she who thought herself ripe for adultery had long grown ready for harlotry" (p. 101). Here Nabokov's editorial comments demonstrate that the laws he is concerned with do not pertain to society but to human consciousness. In terms of these internal laws—as opposed to the public sphere of social convention—Martha's conjugal practices have already descended to a level of experience far baser than that of adultery. Nabokov's emphasis here is on the spirit rather than the letter (or social "label") of Martha's actions. Her marital status does not exempt her from "harlotry"; quite the opposite, Martha's relations with Dreyer are an even bolder form of barter. While the prostitute sells her body with indifference, Martha actively loathes the man whose attentions *she* endures for the sake of material comfort.

A generous, easy-going, totally self-absorbed man, Dreyer has inspired Martha's disgust long before she becomes involved with Franz. Dreyer's behavior, his very existence seem to threaten the tidy blueprint of reality Martha has forged in her mind. Everything about Dreyer offends her rigid sense of propriety. He unsettles the deadly order of her world with "freakish twists" of surprising life. The unexpected, the unusual —hence unique and real—is to Martha an aberration. On the train, for example, she looks on in vexation while Dreyer is reading a book of poetry: "Life should proceed according to plan, straight and strict, without freakish twists and wiggles. An elegant book is all right on a drawing-room table . . . But to imbibe and relish . . . poems, if you please . . . in an expensive binding . . . a person who calls himself a businessman cannot, must not, dare not act like that" (p. 10). A moment earlier, briefly distracted from his reading, Dreyer gazes at the outside world which "avidly, like a playful dog waiting for that moment, darted up to him with a bright bound. But pushing Tom away affectionately, Dreyer again immersed himself in his anthology of verse." For Martha, meanwhile, "that frolicsome radiance was simply the stuffy air in a swaying railway car. It is supposed to be stuffy in a car: that is customary and therefore good" (pp. 9-10). Here, indeed, is a radical inversion of the realist's convincingly rendered, putatively objective environment. Both Dreyer's and Martha's versions of reality are shown to be constructs, or fusions, of mind and matter. The material properties of the compartment are ultimately psychic in nature, taking shape in the consciousness that endows them with personal significance.

In contrast to Martha's dull blueprint, Dreyer's world is as bright and gay as an affectionate puppy. His active perception quickly transforms the outside world into a "playful dog" that he affectionately pushes away. In short order metaphorical Tom will actually materialize in the form of Dreyer's pet Alsatian, whose irrepressible spirits meet with as much disapproval from Martha as Dreyer's own. In the succeeding chapter, Tom will emerge "with a bound from the sunny haze, becoming alive, warm, active, and nearly knocking [Franz] off his chair" (p. 29). Tom's association with Dreyer's sunny and warm disposition continues throughout the novel until Martha, mistakenly anticipating the death of her husband, has the gardener do away with his dog. Like Tom, Dreyer's world is a highly personal metaphor, something intimate and gay, which he has fused from his own loving, if self-centered, attention. Martha's world is no metaphor but a dreary composite drawn from the most accessible and acceptable versions of reality provided by convention. In the railway car Martha is excluded from the "frolicsome radiance" that charms Dreyer in his world; she suffers, instead, the discomfort she expects. To find anything *but* stuffy air in the train's close quarters would constitute a threat to her mental security. According to the same self-defeating principle, Martha is duly irritated by the weather: " 'Autumn, rain,' said Martha slamming her handbag shut. 'Oh, just a drizzle,' Dreyer corrected her softly" (p. 17).

Employing self-conscious artifice to break with the novelist's traditional obligations to reality, Nabokov challenges the "half-hearted materialist" who conceives a split between mind and matter, between consciousness and the allegedly real world of objective fact. He deemed himself an "indivisible monist," and explained the term in this way: "Monism, which implies a oneness of basic reality, is seen to be divisible when, say, 'mind' sneakily splits away from 'matter' in the reasoning of a muddled monist or half-hearted materialist."[15] Because true reality, in Nabokov's view, is the essentially unique re-creation of the world through individual perception, his characters are made accountable for the quality of their reality. True, they are confined within the patterns of literary artifice: the fiction itself is a fusion of the author's individual consciousness and the "matter" it has shaped. Despite the strictures of artifice, however, Nabokov's creatures are shown to possess a certain autonomy with respect to reality that the formal realist may not grant. As the realist labors to create a convincing illusion of objective reality, his tendency is to emphasize the overwhelming historical and social forces that engulf the individual's life. Mary McCarthy's description of *War and Peace* reflects this emphasis: "Indeed, it could be said that the real plot of *War and Peace* is the struggle of the characters not to be immersed, engulfed, swallowed up by the landscape of fact and 'history' in which they, like all human beings, have been placed: freedom (the subjective) is in the fiction, and necessity is in the fact."[16] By demonstrating that each man's world—that privately created construct—is more "subjective" than we commonly think, Nabokov, the alleged literary despot, affords his "galley slaves" a potential freedom that is inaccessible to the characters of formal realism.[17] In the case of Martha and Dreyer, for example, we note that Martha receives from the "anthropomorphic deity" impersonated by Nabokov both the rain and the stuffy air she warrants. These elements of her environment take shape from her character, or psyche, and are part of her fate. Nabokov scrupulously refrains from inflicting them on Dreyer.

In the vastly different landscapes men create for themselves, they may be prisoners or kings. "Physical Franz" is a victim of every passing impression threatening to unleash the "horrors" that lurk in the depths of his passive psyche. Martha is a prisoner in a different sense. While Franz is the slave of claustrophobic sensation, Martha is afflicted by death. As she gazes through the train window at the scenery outside, Martha finds not only Dreyer but the "flicker of woods in the window" highly "irksome." Her bored and loveless spirit creates a virtual prison of her surroundings: "The sun penetrated her eyelids with solid scarlet, across which luminous stripes moved in succession (the ghostly negative of the passing forest), and a replica of her husband's cheerful face, as if slowly rotating toward her, got mixed up in this barred redness, and she opened her eyes with a start" (p. 9). The play of light and shadow here creates "luminous stripes" that suggest the bars of a prison cell.[18] As many critics have pointed out, reflecting surfaces—mirrors, windows, water—frequently signal the operation of consciousness in Nabokov's fiction. The world we perceive is a reflection, made up of images formed by the lens of the eye, conveyed to the retina, and registered in the mind of the observer. The "ghostly negative of the passing forest" reflected on the underside of Martha's lids suggests the deadly world created in her dormant consciousness. Even more striking is the image of Dreyer's "cheerful face" whirling through this "barred redness." As it gets "mixed up" in the ghostly landscape, the face—like a luminous red sun in a Magritte painting—startles Martha out of semi-sleep with its disturbing life. The image later recurs in transmuted form, but with the same disturbing impact, in Franz's myopic and drunken perception: "Dreyer, slowly rotating before him like a flaming wheel with human arms for spokes, began discussing the job awaiting Franz" (p. 37). Even before they have any motive to murder Dreyer, Martha and Franz struggle with the mysterious source of energy that emanates from his vital being.

Dreyer has a lively internal life that remains vexingly inaccessible to Martha's despotic will. Hating him for eluding the strictures of her world as he "removes himself" with a book, Martha initially projects her destructive impulses on the book itself: "How nice it would be to pluck that book out of his hands and lock it up in a suitcase" (p. 10). As Nabokov later demonstrates in *Invitation to a Beheading*, all prison guards partake of Martha's prison mentality; they want to lock up things and people. After she meets Franz, Martha's impulse to get rid of Dreyer's book quickly mushrooms into an obsession to be rid of its reader. Both thing and person become hateful objects, obstacles to her program for existence. With psychological acumen, Nabokov illustrates the murderer's degraded form of logic and its origin in dehumanizing thought. The first stage of murder is always an act of psychological, rather than physical, violence. The murderer's initial assault on his victim takes the form of deadly mental abstraction: "He now stood in her path, in her plain, straight path, like a solid obstacle, that ought somehow to be removed to

34

let her resume her plain straight existence. How dared he enforce upon her the complications of adultery?" (p. 141). Hoping to get rid of this obstacle, Martha mentally reduces her husband to "the thing called Dreyer" (p. 180).

Unaware that his wife is mentally extracting the life from him, Dreyer is preoccupied with more speculative questions concerning life and death. He hires an ingenious Inventor to create lifelike automannequins for his department store. Ultimately, however, the banality of the results leaves him disenchanted with such mechanical reproductions. Dummies prove to be just that: "This time the woman [dummy] drifted past on slow roller skates, . . . her legs rigid, her profile like that of a skull, her décolleté revealing a tricot smudged by the hasty hands of her maker . . . Dreyer wondered what aberration of mind had ever made him accept, let alone admire, those tipsy dummies" (pp. 262-263). For Dreyer, the dummies are hopelessly inert approximations of human vitality. The mystery of creation eludes the mechanical techniques of the Inventor, who "ran into some trouble [with the female dummy], a rib failed to function properly." To Dreyer he quips, "After all, I need more time than God did, Mr. Director" (p. 261). The Inventor attempts to rival God's creation, and fails. Paradoxically, his lackluster female dummy is a striking correlative for Martha's mechanical consciousness—only a shallow approximation of the human.

Despite its mechanical qualities, dehumanized consciousness has an inverse effect on Martha's animal spirits. As her hatred for Dreyer intensifies, Martha's appetite for Franz grows voracious: "She leaned to-

35

NABOKOV AND THE NOVEL

ward him, took the glossy-headed half-bared [chicken] bone out of his hand . . . began gnawing at it with relish . . . her lips growing fuller and brighter" (p. 123). She kisses Franz "as if she were about to give him a gentle bite" and "[takes] possession of his lips." She says to him, "I can certainly touch you, and nibble you, and even swallow you whole if I want" (p. 134). Graphically feeding on Franz's sexual organs, Martha pits their "life" against her husband's. Seated on the bed with naked Franz, she says of Dreyer: "And you know lately he's been so terribly alive. Is he stronger than we? Is he more alive than this, and this, and *this*?" (p. 204). In the course of the novel, Martha becomes a kind of vampire, and "physical Franz" her ghoulish food: "Without his obedient lips and young body she could not live more than a single day" (p. 199).

Whether feeding on her lover's feeble life or devising ways to rid Dreyer of his, Martha is gradually overtaken by the predatory forces of death. Dreyer, meanwhile, continues to relish the abundant signs of life all around him. On his way to view the Inventor's automannequins, he enjoys a walk in the sunlight, exclaiming to himself, "What fun it was to be alive." For him, life is rich in possibility, mystery, and delight: "All those people in the street scurrying by, waiting at streetcar stops: what a bunch of secrets, astonishing professions, incredible recollections" (pp. 205-206). As the murder plot thickens, Martha's strenuous efforts to turn Dreyer into a dummy only dramatize his infinite and inimitable life: "Dreyer was spreading out monstrously before her, like a conflagration in a cinema picture. Human life, like fire, was dangerous and difficult to extinguish; but, as in the case of fire, there must be, there simply must be, some universally accepted, natural method of quenching a man's fierce life . . . Dreyer filled the whole bedroom, the whole house, the whole world" (p. 199).

Before the murderer's shrinking humanity, the vitality of the victim appears to expand limitlessly. Their relationship is, as Charles Kinbote notes in *Pale Fire*, strictly "anti-Darwinian": "The one who kills is *always* his victim's inferior."[19] By depriving his victim of life, the murderer paradoxically forfeits his own powers of vital existence. Gazing at the photographs of numerous murderers, Dreyer notes their "pasty faces" and "the puffy faces of their victims who in death came to resemble them" (p. 207). The victim's corpse is the murderer's true twin, a palpable reflection of his deathly condition. Illustrating this "anti-Darwinian" rule of consciousness, Dreyer, the intended victim, survives the plot while his would-be assassins perish. Martha dies of pneumonia at the end of the novel; long before this, Franz has become a mere automaton: "Vertigo became a habitual and pleasurable state, an automaton's somnambulic languor, the law of his existence" (p. 150).

By consigning his consciousness to Martha's murderous will, Franz does become a kind of puppet, remaining so until Martha's death at the end of the novel. But to regard Franz as a puppet, or "cardboard figure," from the outset—just because he is Nabokov's character, confined to a world of artifice—only blurs the distinctions Nabokov makes throughout the novel between real and simulated human life. Those distinctions are emphasized in the following passage, where Franz thinks to himself:

> There was the dangerous irksome Dreyer who walked, spoke, tormented him, guffawed; and there was a second, purely schematic Dreyer, who had become detached from the first—a stylized playing card, a heraldic design—and it was this that had to be destroyed. Whatever method of annihilation was mentioned, it applied precisely to this schematic image. This Dreyer number two was very convenient to manipulate. He was two-dimensional and immobile. (Pp. 177-178)

Here, in tracing the process of Franz's thoughts, Nabokov clearly suggests that *murder*, not artifice, is the deadly design, the game of deathly abstraction by which Martha and Franz dehumanize Dreyer and, as a result, destroy their own humanity.[20]

While the work of artifice demands the exercise of imagination, murder is, in Nabokov's view, a matter of cliché. When devising her scheme to kill Dreyer, Martha rehearses "the details of elaborate and nonsensical shootings described in trashy novelettes, . . . thereby plagiarizing villainy (an act which after all had been avoided only by Cain)" (p. 178). Murder is derivative and, when compared to the creative acts of consciousness, "essentially boring": Dreyer "was thinking what a talentless person one must be, what a poor thinker or hysterical fool, to murder one's neighbor . . . How much those simpletons were missing! Missing . . . the simple pleasure of existence" (p. 207). In Nabokov's view, the murder-thriller is as banal a literary form as the brutal act on which it depends for its meager effects. In *King, Queen, Knave*, Nabokov exposes the psychological realities of murder that are ignored and falsified in the conventional thriller and, Nabokov might have added, even in celebrated works of fiction like Dostoevsky's *Crime and Punishment*. On more than one occasion Nabokov expressed his impatience with Dostoevsky's "sensitive murderers and soulful prostitutes."[21] One may not agree with Nabokov's dismissal of Dostoevsky, but the principle operating behind his mockery is a serious one. To Nabokov, any writer who encourages the reader's identification with the murderer's psychology is a misguided thinker and a poor artist. In *King, Queen, Knave*, therefore, Nabokov deploys the strategies of artifice to distance the reader from Martha's murderous intentions and, at the same time, to distinguish between the murderer's stock notions and the creative qualities of true consciousness.

Like the murder-thriller, a "sensitive murderer" is, in Nabokov's view, a contradiction in terms. In Dreyer, however, Nabokov created a character who may appear, to some readers, to be an even greater contradiction: a sensitive businessman. Although Dreyer has a supreme talent for making money, he is shown, oddly enough, to be relatively uninterested in it. In Dreyer's case, Nabokov characteristically reverses the novelist's traditional depiction of the ambitious entrepreneur. Dreyer grows rich as a result of the free play of his imagination, not from tightfisted greed. "With miraculous ease" Dreyer makes half his fortune "in a year of freakish luck—at a time when luck, a light touch, and his special kind of imagination were needed" (pp. 65, 195). Contradicting the formulas of nineteenth-century novelists, whereby new wealth burgeons from ruthless exploitation, Dreyer again emerges as an individual rather than a social type, or "label." Nabokov's depiction of Dreyer may not be statistically representative, but it reveals something about human psychology that is nevertheless true: man's success in the world derives from his ability to reformulate the problems inherent in reality with a fresh exercise of perception. Like a scientist, a thinker, or an artist, Dreyer is successful in the practical world because of his psychic detachment from its daily strictures and demands. For him, "the world stands like a dog pleading to be played with" (p. 177). Dreyer's relative lack of interest in money per se allows him to play effectively with it. As a corollary, Martha's material greed makes her despise the very inventiveness that has made her rich. She "loathed her husband's whimsical levity (even though it had once helped him to become rich)" (p. 195).

When Dreyer takes Franz to his department store for a lesson in salesmanship, the lesson is no lesson at all, as it exceeds any possibility for practical imitation by Franz: "And it was not on personal experience, not on the recollection of distant days when he actually had worked behind the counter, that Dreyer drew that night as he showed Franz how to sell neckties. Instead, he soared into the ravishing realm of inutile imagination, demonstrating not the way ties should be sold in real life, but the way they might be sold if the salesman were both artist and clairvoyant" (pp. 69-70). Despite the lesson's lack of utilitarian applicability, Dreyer captures the essence of the daily magic of buying and selling. It is the magic by which human fantasies imbue material objects with enchantments men themselves have created. Materialism is, in this sense, a degraded form of romanticism; things are worshiped as the means to purchasable happiness. Intuitively understanding this, every good salesman has something of the conjuror about him. Thus Dreyer instructs, "Hypnotize [the customer] with the flip of the tie you display. You must make it *bloom* before the idiot's eyes" (p. 71).

Vladislav Khodasevich, the Russian émigré poet and critic, includes Dreyer among the numerous protagonists in Nabokov's Russian fiction whose occupations—as businessman or chess-player, for example—are only "masks" for that of the artist. As a boy, Dreyer did dream of becoming an artist (p. 223); but casting him in the role of "genuine, inspired artist," to quote Khodasevich, does not satisfactorily account for his fully realized existence as a character.[22] What happens to Dreyer in the novel partly arises from the way he demonstrably *differs from* a practicing artist, especially from the artist who created him. Dreyer's failure to become an artist is specifically linked to his psychological makeup. He himself wonders *why* he cannot break away from his present mode of life as a businessman: "What prevented him from seeing the world? He had the means—but there was some fatal veil between him and every dream that beckoned him. He was a bachelor with a beautiful marble wife, a passionate hobbyist without anything to collect, an explorer not knowing on what mountain to die, a voracious reader of unmemorable books, a happy and healthy failure" (pp. 223-224). The very form of Dreyer's unwitting thoughts here reveals his misconceptions about reality. He wonders, for example, why he cannot "see the world." The idiomatic expression suggests that Dreyer fails to envision the world sufficiently, and his failure somehow prevents him from entering upon a freer mode of existence. We know, of course, that Dreyer's "beautiful marble wife" is no such thing; Martha is avidly sexual and only appears to be made of marble because she despises her husband. We recall, too, that one of the "unmemorable books" Dreyer has been reading is a classic of Russian literature: "*Die toten Seelen* [*Dead Souls*] by a Russian author, which had long been slipping down Dreyer's knee, slid onto the flags of the floor, and he felt too lazy to pick it up" (p. 43). If Dreyer were a less lazy "reader," he might have discovered in Gogol's rendering of banal evil and spiritless existence a key to the behavior of his own wife.[23] Dreyer, however, is not a vigilant enough "explorer" of reality to see that there are mountains to scale right where he is.

The "fatal veil" that comes between Dreyer and his dreams is also the veil that prevents him from seeing deeply enough into the human beings around him. Dreyer is an amiable solipsist and a poor psychologist. His former mistress Erica chides him for turning the people in his life into flat characters: "You seat a person on a little shelf and think she'll keep sitting like that forever." Accusing him of "skimming along the surface" of reality, she suggests that Dreyer has no idea what his wife is really like: "You love her— oh, ardently—and don't bother about what she's like inside." Erica guesses that Martha is deceiving him, but Dreyer insists that Martha "does not know the first letter of adultery," adding that she "is not what you'd call a passionate woman" (p. 175). The "fatal veil" blurring Dreyer's perception, and nearly proving fatal to his life, is a "neutral film of familiarity" that clouds his vision: "Luckily for Franz, his observant uncle's interest in any object, animated or not, whose distinctive features he had immediately grasped, or thought he had grasped, gloated over and filed away, would wane with its every subsequent reappearance. The bright perception became the habitual abstraction . . . It was too boring to think that the object might change of its own accord and assume unforeseen characteristics. That would mean having to enjoy it again, and he was no longer young" (p. 106). Along with his "distant, thrifty, frigid wife" of seven years, Dreyer seats Franz on a mental shelf "amid the rest of the familiar objects and people" (pp. 106, 217).

The gradual dimming of perception is the bane of any artist. The veil of familiarity, as Wordsworth among others recognized, obstructs creative vision. The artist consolidates his energies to combat the process by which "bright perception" fades into "habitual abstraction." As the partial author of his world, Dreyer grows complacent, tending to make still-shots of once living impressions and flat characters of other people. Content with his first impressions of Martha and Franz, he does not question the truth of his "initial concept." In his mind their images "simply became more compactly filled up with fitting characteristics" (p. 106). While waiting in the local courthouse, Dreyer keenly perceives the spiritual death lurking in the "pasty faces" of numberless murderers. When he returns home, however, he fails to detect that same deathly pallor in the faces of Martha and Franz. The manner in which they await him strikes the reader, who is "in the know," as ominous, indeed. Dreyer, however, is reassured, incorrectly, by their familiarity: "They were standing motionless side by side, watching him approach. And he felt a pleasant relief at seeing at last two familiar, two perfectly human faces" (p. 209). While Dreyer assumes, quite naturally, that his wife and nephew are perfectly human, Nabokov supplies evidence that radically contradicts this point of view.

In the Nabokovian artifice, human existence is clearly a psychic matter. Within the frame of the fiction, claiming no existence beyond the artifice of imagination, Nabokov's characters are "real" only in terms of the conscious life they exhibit. Those who are shown to ignore the "calling and rank" of conscious, specifically human life may descend to inhuman or subhuman status. Thus, on occasion, even Franz's dull mind gleans the truth about Martha. Her obsession with murder has transformed her into "a large white toad" (pp. 198, 259). Here Martha takes her place among those other Nabokovian creations from whom ultimate humanity is stringently withheld: Cincinnatus's absurd jailers in *Invitation to a Beheading*; the dummy-dictator Paduk in *Bend Sinister*; and Gradus, John Shade's lethal but essentially unreal assassin in *Pale Fire*. Mechanically pursuing a "clean, honest, orderly course of death," Gradus, for example, is only a "clockwork man": "He could read, write and reckon, he was endowed with a modicum of self-awareness (with which he did not know what to do), some duration consciousness, and a good memory for faces, names, dates and the like. Spiritually he did not exist. Morally he was a dummy pursuing another dummy."[24] Gradus's reduction to the spiritual status of "dummy" reminds us of the Inventor's automannequins, whose crude simulation of the human proves so disenchanting to Dreyer. In both cases, Nabokov distinguishes between the reflexes of mechanical existence and the complex processes by which a vitally engaged mind, heart, or soul manifests real life. Having abandoned those complex processes, Gradus and Martha are demoted from the "calling and rank" of true human existence. Agents of dehumanized consciousness, they sink to the subhuman level of their own base perceptions. Morally dead, the murderers inevitably take their place among the other dummies that populate the assassin's deathly landscape. According to the same moral logic, Nabokov once assessed the "metempsychic sloth" of a drug addict he knew: "He must be grazing today on some grassy slope in Tibet if he has not yet lined the coat of the fortunate shepherd."[25] The tone of his dismissal may strike us as highly unsympathetic, but Nabokov's disdain clearly derives from his scrupulous and unremitting attention to what *is* human in our creatural existence. The image of the grazing sheep bears witness to the addict's wholesale abdication from the operations of consciousness.

The distinctions Nabokov makes between apparent and real human nature are, as in Dreyer's case, more accessible to his readers than to his characters. Within the matrix of his own existence, and despite his lively curiosity, Dreyer succumbs to the natural tendency to fit reality to his habitual assumptions. While his failure to perceive the truth about his wife and her lover tells us a good deal about Dreyer's own nature, his shortsightedness also suggests some essential differences between the spheres of literature and life. Clairvoyance, our ability to "see into" other people, is, after all, a condition more readily achieved in art than in life. The people we live with are never, for all their apparent familiarity, as completely imagined and understood as those we read about in novels. The products of intense acts of creative consciousness, literary characters are imagined into being by the author and then reimagined by the reader. If the novelist has done his work, his characters will form more complete and coherent images in our minds than the partial pictures we haphazardly construct of each other. Our vision of reality, and of each other, is always partial and imperfect. Only in fiction can imagination and experience create a whole. The "whole story" eludes us in our lives; yet we demand it of the fiction we read.

While Nabokov's character Dreyer may, in some ways, resemble an artist or an artist *manqué*, there is no mistaking his inadequacy as the author's purported "mask" or stand-in. Nor are the limitations of Dreyer's vision and insight to be considered as signs of his author's arrogance toward human beings. Dreyer's inferiority to his creator is, quite simply, a truthful reflection of the laws of all creation. While each man is the partial author of his private world— creating and recreating the landscape from his consciousness *of* it—he is not the Author of the entire universe he shares with others. Nabokov and his readers are privy, therefore, to secrets that escape his characters' active but limited perceptions. Dreyer remains ignorant of the essential nature of his wife, his nephew, and the plot arranged between them. Meanwhile, in the foreword to the American edition of *King, Queen, Knave,* the author identifies the characters who are his true representatives in the novel. In the final chapters of the book, Nabokov points out, he and his wife make "visits of inspection" to the seaside resort where the novel's dénouement occurs (foreword, p. viii). There, on the beach, Franz is appropriately discomfited by the sensation that this foreign couple knows "absolutely everything about his predicament" (p. 259).

Self-conscious artifice, I hope it is clear, does not eliminate reality from Nabokov's novels but reveals it in new ways. Because consciousness is "the only real thing in the world and the greatest mystery of all," Nabokov's artifice reflects not the world so much as the process by which men call it into being. That process is both psychic in nature and psychologically revealing. "All novelists of any worth," Nabokov said, "are psychological novelists," because "the shifts of levels, the interpenetration of successive impressions . . . belong of course to psychology—psychology at its best."[26] Here, certainly, Nabokov gives no indication that his protagonists are meant to serve as mere masks for the artist who created them. In his fiction, as well, Nabokov's emphasis is not on the exclusive enterprise of the artist but on the essentially *creative* processes of consciousness—psychology in action and "at its best." Human reality is a construct, an incomplete but wholly significant fusion of individual

47

perception with the phenomenological world. By drawing attention to the frame of his fiction, Nabokov does more than remind us we are reading a book. He reminds us that *reading* the world is the central preoccupation, and prerogative, of human beings. It is only in the realm of "articulate art," to borrow Humbert's phrase, that we mortals can hope to transcend the partial vision of our own psychic landscape —to contemplate, and share with the author, the lucid design of an entire universe. Here the novelist is godlike, ready to present to his readers the whole story of his creation. We are given to recognize how everything in this delightfully artificial universe has been thoroughly imagined, crafted, and imbued with the values of consciousness. The origins and mysteries of such a world are made accessible to the reader who exerts himself. Articulation—the strategies of composition—demands the vigilant exercise of consciousness, which in turn requires vigilant perception to be grasped. In Nabokov's view, good art is always difficult, unnatural, and strange. By celebrating, and affirming, the highest aspirations of conscious life, good art will always disturb or elude minds that are ready to accept and be ruled by the reflexes of habit.

CHAPTER III

Breaking the Law of Averages: *Invitation to a Beheading*

Invitation to a Beheading (1938), the next-to-last novel Nabokov wrote in Russian, has often been compared by critics and by Nabokov himself to his second novel in English, *Bend Sinister* (1947). In the author's words, they are "the two bookends of grotesque design between which my other volumes tightly huddle."[1] Though they occupy the chronological center of Nabokov's entire *oeuvre*, they were stationed, in Nabokov's imagination, at either end of a hypothetical shelf—each with a side fully exposed to the outside world. The image is apt, because in both novels the main characters are more cruelly exposed to the harsh pressures of the external environment than in any of Nabokov's other fiction. The "grotesque design" of these "bookends" reflects the absurd and terrifying involutions of collective life in its most pernicious form—the totalitarian regime. The potential adversary relationship between the state and the individual here becomes one of outright hostility, for the regime is murderously opposed to the real life of consciousness. As my discussion of *Invitation* and of *Bend Sinister* in the succeeding chapter should make clear, Nabokov recognized that the individual's "inner disentanglement" from the pressures and assumptions of collective life is, like the condition of clairvoyance, more readily achieved in art than in life. It is only within the context of literary artifice, therefore, that he affirms the absolute power of human consciousness over the onerous forces of the material environment. An "individual monist," Nabokov would not have approved of the arbitrary distinction I have just made between psychic and material reality. Therefore I should like to restate that distinction in terms he favored—the distinction between "average reality" and "true reality."

"Average reality" is the public realm shared by the individuals who make up a society. Contributing to this domain are the social concerns, political anxieties, and financial crises that plague every generation of men and women, consuming a great deal of their attention and energy. Despite its practical power and temporal prestige, "average reality" is for Nabokov an inferior realm, not "true reality." It is "only the reality of general ideas, conventional forms of humdrummery, current editorials."[2] This general world of common causes promotes the lowest common denominator—the average—of individual human consciousness. It is always being added up and accounted for by the sociologist, the psychologist, and the reporter. Collective life is always a compromise, and the general notion of the "common man" only a caricature of the individual's specific nature.

Nabokov was not, however, naïvely unaware of the power that collective society wields over the individual. Describing himself as "an old-fashioned liberal,"[3] he regarded democracy as the political and social system best suited to the individual's unique needs and talents:

> The splendid paradox of democracy is that while stress is laid on the rule of all and equality of common rights, it is the individual that derives from it his special and uncommon benefit. Ethically, the members of a democracy are equals; spiritually, each has the right to be as different from his neighbors as he pleases . . . Democracy is humanity at its best, not because we happen to think that a republic is better than a king and a king is better than nothing and nothing is better than a dictator, but because it is the natural condition of every man since the human mind became conscious not only of the world but of itself. Morally, democracy is invincible. Physically, that side will win which has the better guns.[4]

In every society, those who vigilantly promote the laws and conventions by which it operates have a vested interest in doing so. Because conscious life naturally exposes the inferior aspects of average reality, those in power will inevitably be hostile to its uninhibited operation. In all societies this is true to some extent. But the leaders of totalitarian societies can least afford this kind of exposure and therefore have the least tolerance for it. Private thought becomes the public enemy, as Nabokov illustrates in both *Invitation to a Beheading* and *Bend Sinister*. In the totalitarian state, the opposition between the deadening norms of convention and the vitality of creative sensibility becomes an out-and-out struggle between the public and private realms of existence—between average reality and true reality. The machinery of the state uses attrition, coercion, and torture to wage war on an elusive psychic process, the free play of consciousness. In many ways, the contest is logically absurd. The ineffable nature of thought inevitably eludes the material power of the state that it threatens. Attempting to locate and destroy the source of free thought, the totalitarian machine is as clumsy as it is brutal.

In *Invitation to a Beheading*, the absurdity of totalitarian logic is manifested in a farcical prison setting. The fortress in which Cincinnatus C., the protagonist, finds himself is a blatant sham, as trumped up as the charge against him: Cincinnatus is found guilty of "gnostical turpitude," having committed, it seems, the foul crime of possessing a soul. Every prison is a paradox when we consider the internal freedoms of consciousness. While the jailers lock up the prisoner's body and dictate the physical conditions of his existence, no prison can effectively control the activities of the mind and imagination. The ridiculous guards in *Invitation* are busy spying on Cincinnatus's most trivial physical act, but they haven't a clue how to inhibit the "criminal exercise" in which he spontaneously engages. Even in his cell Cincinnatus continues the illegal activity for which he has been jailed; he subversively exercises his imagination and thought whenever the spirit moves him.

The contradiction between man's finite and frail body and his potentially infinite conscious life accounts for the paradox of the prison. In *Speak, Memory*, Nabokov describes the "infinity of sensation and thought" which consciousness develops "within a finite existence."[5] Tolstoy engages this paradox in *War and Peace*, when Pierre considers his situation as a prisoner of the French troops:

> He . . . sat motionless for a long time, thinking. More than an hour passed. No one disturbed Pierre. Suddenly he burst out with his thick, good-natured laugh—so loudly that from every direction people looked around with surprise at this strange, evidently solitary laughter.
> "Ha, ha, ha," laughed Pierre. And he began to talk aloud to himself: "The soldier didn't let me pass. They caught me, locked me up. They're keeping me in captivity. Whom? Me? Me—my immortal soul. Ha, ha, ha," he laughed, tears having sprung to his eyes . . .
> Pierre glanced at the sky, into the depths of the receding stars at play. "And all this is mine, and all this is in me, and all this is I," thought Pierre. "And all this they have caught and shut up in a stall, fenced off with planks." He smiled and walked off to his comrades to lie down to sleep.[6]

Viktor Shklovsky included this passage among the "several hundred" that, he said, illustrate the technique of *ostranenie*, or defamiliarization, in Tolstoy's fiction. Although he did not explicate this passage, Shklovsky's point is self-evident. Pierre's reaction to the phenomenon of captivity is rendered in an unfamiliar light. Instead of despairing, in this moment of captivity, at his loss of freedom, he experiences an intense sensation of spiritual freedom. No "half-hearted materialist," to repeat Nabokov's phrase, Pierre suddenly recognizes the essential "oneness" of his mind with the material universe embraced by "the arms of consciousness." The sky and "the depths of the receding stars" are perceived by Pierre and as such they belong, irrevocably, to him. They are elements of his existence. No material prison can bar Pierre from the infinite reaches of his own perception, memory, and imagination. Thus Pierre's physical captivity ceases, at this moment, to frighten him; and he smiles in irony at these local bonds.

This affinity between Tolstoy's eminently realistic great novel and Nabokov's *Invitation* suggests, once again, how Nabokov's "aesthetic" artifice may embody and develop the traditionally humanistic concerns of the novel while breaking with its formal conventions. Alfred Appel, Jr., has said that in *Invitation* Nabokov develops the absurd logic of the police state into "an extreme and fantastic metaphor for the imprisonment of the mind, thus making consciousness, rather than politics, the subject of [this novel]."[7] Nabokov is able to locate Cincinnatus's struggle within the psyche, rather than in social reality, because artifice here serves to discredit the reality of the prison itself. It is blatantly inauthentic, a fake; its "credibility" is not literal and objectively convincing but wholly dependent on Cincinnatus's subjective participation in its staged illusion. His confinement depends on his own acquiescence in the role of prisoner, accepting as real the police state's absurd pretensions to controlling a man's "immortal soul" as well as his body. Only at the end of the novel does Cincinnatus joyfully achieve "a clarity [of mind] he had never experienced before," recognizing like Pierre the true nature of his indestructible freedom.[8]

For Nabokov, the "so-called 'realism' of old novels" falsely promotes average reality as though it were true reality. Such novels employ "vulgar clichés," "social comment," and "journalistic generalities" to promote their own authenticity. To this banal and "boring" presentation of reality, "faked by a mediocre performer," Nabokov opposed the "real, authentic" nature of "imaginary worlds," that is, fictions.[9] In *Invitation*, this contrast between obvious but fake reality and dreamy but difficult truth is extensively developed. Cincinnatus is an imaginative dreamer whose consciousness becomes the locus of reality in an otherwise fake world. The novel's title is not the only aspect of the novel that reverses our conventional expectations (the beheading does not even take place). Neither the setting, the secondary characters, nor even Cincinnatus's dramatic plight contributes to a sustained illusion of authenticity.

"The novel," says Mary McCarthy, "does not permit occurrences outside the order of nature—miracles." Moreover, "the characters in a novel must obey the laws of nature. They cannot blow up . . . or rise from the dead, as they can in plays."[10] In a flagrant reversal of these facts of (novelistic) life, Nabokov permits Cincinnatus to rise from the execution block, in sheer defiance of the axe's death-blow and all reasonable expectations. Meanwhile the creaky theatrics of staged "average reality" perish in Cincinnatus's place:

> The spectators were quite transparent, and quite useless, and they all kept surging and moving away—only the back rows, being painted rows, remained in place. Cincinnatus slowly descended from the platform and walked off through the shifting debris. He

was overtaken by Roman, who was now many times smaller and who was at the same time Rodrig: "What are you doing!" he croaked, jumping up and down. "You can't, you can't! It's dishonest toward him, toward everybody . . . Come back, lie down—after all, you were lying down, everything was ready, everything was finished!" (Pp. 222-223)

In *Invitation*, the time-honored devices employed by a realist to secure the credibility of his fictional world are so flagrantly installed and deliberately mismanaged that they parody their conventional functions. In every novel, for example, time must pass; and so, as E. M. Forster said, "there is always a clock."[11] The narrative, in other words, requires a coherent time-scheme that sensibly orders events, even if those events are not chronologically reported. In *Invitation*, a prison clock noisily marks the passing of story time, while a spider, fed by the jailer, spins out its insinuating thread: "A clock struck—four or five times—with the vibrations and re-vibrations, and reverberations proper to a prison. Feet working, a spider—official friend of the jailed—lowered itself on a thread from the ceiling" (p. 13). Far from introducing a coherent time-scheme naturally within the novel, Nabokov emphasizes the artificial presence of both clock and spider. They are not meant to create a convincing impression of time's progress but to announce themselves with appropriate fanfare, as adjuncts of the setting. All prisons, after all, run on time; and all prisoners are made to serve it.

The fortress in which Cincinnatus is held prisoner is as trumped up as the noisy clock and the well-fed spider. The walls of the fortress look freshly painted, as though hastily improvised for the purposes of the plot. When Cincinnatus's mother visits him in prison, he accuses her of playing a role in a mediocre stage production: "And why is your raincoat wet when your shoes are dry—see, that's careless. Tell the prop man for me" (p. 132). On the eve of his impending execution, the carpenters are still knocking together the appropriate prop—in this case, the platform on which the prisoner is to be beheaded: "A blunt knock-knock-knock came from somewhere off to the left as they were descending Steep Avenue. Knock-knock-knock. 'The scoundrels,' muttered M'sieur Pierre, 'Didn't they swear it was all done?' " (pp. 190-191). Each time that Rodion, the jailer, opens Cincinnatus's cell, he has to struggle with the "wrong key," and only a fuss or a "potent bit of Russian swearing" turns "the trick" (pp. 11, 60). From all evidence, it appears that the novel's setting is itself a kind of staged theatrical "trick." The jailer Rodion, the lawyer Roman, and the prison director Rodrig are decked out in costumes contrived for a theatrical production. The lawyer wears "a frock coat, with a smudge on his celluloid collar and an edging of pinkish muslin at the back of his head where the black wig ended" (p. 40). Their roles, like their names, are interconnected. Rodion repeatedly drops his red wig on a chair and turns into the prison director, who finishes up the sweeping. At one point, Rodion, Roman, and Cincinnatus leave the cell and climb to the top of the fortress. The "same little procession" starts back—only this time, Rodrig, Roman, and Cincinnatus return. In one sentence Rodion disappears, and in another his broom materializes in the hands of the director, who,

57

"tossing the broom in a corner," puts on his frock coat (p. 44). The uniform identity of Cincinnatus's jailers is clearly visible when they fail to put on their makeup: "Haggard, pallid, . . . without any makeup, without padding and without wigs, with rheumy eyes, . . . they turned out to resemble each other, and their identical heads moved identically on their thin necks" (p. 207). Warden, jailer, lawyer—they form three identical links in the chain that binds Cincinnatus to impending doom. Doom, in the form of a death sentence, is announced in the novel's opening line: "In accordance with the law the death sentence was announced to Cincinnatus C. in a whisper."

A condemned man, Cincinnatus is expected, nonetheless, to comply with "the law." Admonishing Cincinnatus for his lack of public spirit, the prison director chides, "You ought to be more cooperative, mister" (p. 39). The prison rules, tacked to the wall of Cincinnatus's cell, are meant to prohibit not only the prisoner's actions but his dreams: "It is desirable that the inmate should not have at all, or if he does, should immediately himself suppress nocturnal dreams whose content might be incompatible with the condition and status of the prisoner, such as: resplendent landscapes, outings with friends, family dinners, as well as sexual intercourse with persons who in real life and in the waking state would not suffer said individual to come near" (p. 49). This absurd rule could not, of course, be enforced by any regime, no matter the number and size of its henchmen. The jailers' comical attempt to enlist the dreamer's cooperation with "the law" betrays their frustration with regard to the freedoms of psychic life. Eluding the

58

dictates of the public sphere, human dreams are inherently subversive.

When appeals to the prisoner's public spirit fail, the executioner, Monsieur Pierre, appeals to Cincinnatus's common sense: " 'Come, come, what kind of nonsense is that?' said M'sieur Pierre, squirming in his chair. 'Only in fairy tales do people escape from prison' " (p. 114). Purporting to be a realist, M'sieur Pierre insists that novelistic events must appear to develop in a probable way from familiar causes. He knows that realistic fiction tends to subordinate improbable, or fanciful, effects to the creation of a plausible world of apparently natural laws, thereby ensuring its credibility. But M'sieur Pierre's "realistic" attitude deliberately excludes from consideration his author's radical approach to reality. Parodying the devices novelists use to establish the credit of their fictional worlds, Nabokov devalues every aspect of his novel except the improbable dreams, perceptions, and memories of his protagonist. When, for example, Cincinnatus's mother visits him in his cell, he accuses her of being a fraud: "I can see perfectly well that you are just as much of a parody as everybody and everything else" (p. 132). On the other hand, what strikes Cincinnatus as real is the fleeting expression of human tenderness he detects in his mother's eyes: "He suddenly noticed the expression in Cecilia C.'s eyes— just for an instant, an instant—but it was as if something real, unquestionable (in this world, where everything was subject to question), had passed through, as if a corner of this horrible life had curled up, and there was a glimpse of the lining" (p. 136). The apparition of love or sympathy that Cincinnatus glimpses in his mother's eyes, or imagines he glimpses there, or imagines he glimpses in the eyes of a woman impersonating his mother, or in the eyes of an apparition conjured from memory—that is reality. Meanwhile, the elaborate props, the setting, the various roles being noisily enacted around him are a fake. It is only "average reality," organized for the consumption of the average man—that caricature of a real man—who has here become a blatant parody. Cincinnatus, in a flash of understanding, will finally extricate himself from this nightmarish law of averages. Addressing the parodies of this sham world, he will declare, "I am not an ordinary—I am the one among you who is alive" (p. 52). And then he will prove what he says.

In the invented world of *Invitation*, unconvincing versions of natural laws are transcended by eminently literary ones. Nabokov's artifice is a literary landscape reflecting the psychological state of Cincinnatus's perception. Musing about his wife, Marthe, Cincinnatus demonstrates his basic understanding of this principle at work: "Her world. Her world consists of simple components, simply joined; I think that the simplest cook-book recipe is more complicated than the world she bakes as she hums: every day for herself, for me, for everyone" (p. 63). Similarly, as the fortress's "sole prisoner," Cincinnatus is its *raison d'être*; the "dummy" officials depend on this construct for their identities. They are mere products of the environment, but Cincinnatus is not. As the prison's only human representative, the only one "who is alive," Cincinnatus is uniquely responsible for the environment that holds him prisoner. A striking contrast between two perspectives of the Tamara Gardens helps to illustrate this point.

In the Tamara Gardens Cincinnatus once wooed his beloved and unfaithful wife, Marthe. To his lonely and unhappy heart, the gardens now beckon with the charm of romantic yesterdays and tomorrows. The "glimmer and haze" of the gardens and "the dove-blue melting hills beyond them" form the distant horizon for which the prisoner longs, with "ineffably vague and perhaps even blissful despair" (p. 43). The first perspective occurs on the eve of Cincinnatus's intended execution. He leaves the prison to attend a "farewell" party considerately thrown in his honor by the prison officials. On a porch, peering into darkness, Cincinnatus suddenly realizes that he is "in the very thick" of his beloved gardens. Despite the night that makes everything invisible, he fully envisions them:

> Now, exploring the surroundings with a diligent eye, he easily removed the murky film of night from the familiar lawns and also erased from them the superfluous lunar dusting, so as to make them exactly as they were in his memory. As he restored the painting smudged by the soot of night, he saw groves, paths, brooks taking shape where they used to be . . . In the distance, pressing against the metallic sky, the charmed hills stood still, glossed with blue and folded in gloom. (P. 187)

At midnight on the same night, the officials gather for a special treat devised by the prison's chief engineer. He has arranged for hundreds of lamps to stud the Tamara Gardens and illumine the night. Here is the second perspective: "The guests applauded. For three minutes a good million light bulbs of diverse colors burned, artfully planted in the grass, in branches, on cliffs, and all arranged in such a way as to embrace the whole nocturnal landscape with a grandiose monogram of 'P' and 'C', which, however, had not quite come off. Thereupon the lights went out all at once and solid darkness reached up to the terrace" (p. 189). The engineers of the beheading plot attempt to fasten the chain that binds Cincinnatus to his executioners. They only manage, however, a mechanical lighting trick that flickers and fades. By contrast, the gardens' real illumination results from Cincinnatus's loving evocation. Only Cincinnatus's consciousness can illumine the literary landscape and give it life.

At times Cincinnatus understands the nature of his special powers, but fear of death persistently clouds his perception. Then he begins, with awesome vitality, to reconstruct the absurd prison as a terrible Gothic dungeon, just as he evokes, so rhapsodically, the Tamara Gardens. Both fortress and gardens ultimately exist in the melting blue haze of Cincinnatus's subjective perception. Even the lawyer's "made-up face" has "dark blue eyebrows" (p. 37), while Pierre, the executioner, first appears "all frosted with gloss, melting just a little in the shaft of sunlight falling on him from above" (p. 59). The toy ball that belongs to the prison director's daughter is also a "glossy red and blue" (p. 41).

The true reality of the prison depends in a special way on Cincinnatus's own attitude toward it. Without his cooperation, so urgently desired by the officials, it remains shadowy and unconvincing. The parodies become real only when Cincinnatus evokes them with dangerous intensity. Then he invests the flimsy setting with a significance it otherwise lacks and inspires the puppets with life:

> Cincinnatus spent this night in a mental review of the hours he had passed in the fortress. Involuntarily yielding to the temptation of logical development, involuntarily (be careful, Cincinnatus!) forging into a chain all the things that were quite harmless as long as they remained unlinked, he inspired the meaningless with meaning, and the lifeless with life. With the stone darkness for background he now permitted the spotlighted figures of all his usual visitors to appear —it was the very first time that his imagination was so condescending toward them. (P. 155)

The intensity of Cincinnatus's psychic "condescension" nearly establishes the authenticity of a literary hoax. Instead of negotiating Cincinnatus's adjustment to this "invented habitus" (p. 36), the author warns him to be careful. He understands the power of consciousness to credit and transform an inferior world: "By evoking them—not believing in them, perhaps, but still evoking them—Cincinnatus allowed them the right to exist, supported them, nourished them with himself" (p. 156). The exercise of perception is, for Cincinnatus, clearly a life-and-death matter. At this perilous moment, the prison clock begins to strike with "mounting exultation" (p. 156), and it appears that Cincinnatus will succumb to "the law" of the theatrical plot. The clock, however, is ultimately disappointed. At the close of the novel— his delicate, sensitive head already poised on the executioner's block—Cincinnatus abruptly rises and reflects: "Why am I here? Why am I lying down like this?" Having asked this simple but essential question, he takes a good look around: "Little was left of the square . . . The fallen trees lay flat and reliefless, while those that were still standing, also two-dimensional, . . . barely held on with their branches to the ripping mesh of the sky. Everything was coming apart. Everything was falling. A spinning wind was picking up and whirling: dust, rags, chips of painted wood, bits of gilded plaster, pasteboard bricks, posters" (p. 223). At his challenge, the fake scenery collapses; and Cincinnatus, against all probability, departs.

"Average reality," said Nabokov, "begins to rot and stink as soon as the act of individual creation ceases to animate a subjectively perceived texture."[12] This "rot and stink" is a symptom of moral decay; and any public reality that claims the individual's participation but is no longer tolerant of his individuality suffers from this moral rot. Such a society becomes essentially unreal, and exists only through lies, tricks, and brute power. In *Invitation to a Beheading*, collective society, represented by the prison officials, has outlawed Cincinnatus's acts of individual creation and intends to remove the source of the subversion—Cincinnatus's head. Masking brutal intention with the guise of public spirit, genteel M'sieur Pierre glorifies the impending execution: "Let the will of the public be carried out!" (p. 175). Cincinnatus must either surrender his head to the state or withdraw its life-giving capacity for consciousness from the mediocre production that is lifeless without it. Instead of crediting the subhuman parodies with life, Cincinnatus puts his head to better use and holds on to it. He finds the trappings of the prison and its functionaries to be beneath credibility, and refuses to play a leading role in such an awful production.

In *The Gulag Archipelago*, Alexander Solzhenitsyn describes Russia's political trials in the twenties and thirties as "theatrical productions" staged at the dictator's will for his own mad purposes. Solzhenitsyn's point is that the entire society of Stalinist Russia was in the grip of a madman whose destructive acts were paraded as manifestations of the public will, carried out for the public good. Behind the rigged stage, Stalin was pulling all the strings, and human beings either became his puppets or were destroyed (or both). Thus far I have been describing Nabokov's radically individualistic attitude toward "average reality" as inherently opposed to notions of historical fate and social identity. But in the context of a rotting social reality, Cincinnatus's kind of psychic revolt may be regarded as historically profound in its own way. What was desperately lacking in Stalinist Russia, Solzhenitsyn tells us, was the individual act of imaginative revolt. The assertion of personal identity could have discredited the totalitarian fraud. In his description, Solzhenitsyn employs images strikingly similar to the ones developed more than forty years ago by Nabokov in *Invitation*. In this context, Cincinnatus's refusal to surrender his personal identity to the trumped up "will of the public" becomes, in Solzhenitsyn's words, an act of profound "historical comprehension":

> It was all that same invincible theme song, persisting with only minor variations through so many different trials: *"After all, we and you are Communists!*

How could you have gotten off the track and come out against us? Repent! After all, you and we together— is *us!"*

Historical comprehension ripens slowly in a society. And when it does ripen, it is so simple. Neither in 1922, nor in 1924, nor in 1937 were the defendants able to hang onto their own point of view so firmly that they could raise their heads and shout, in reply to that bewitching and anesthetizing melody:

"No, we are not revolutionaries *with you!* No, we are not Russians *with you!* No, we are not Communists *with you!"*

It would seem that if only that kind of shout had been raised, all the stage sets would have collapsed, the plaster masks would have fallen off, the Producer [Stalin] would have fled down the backstairs, and the prompters would have sneaked off into their ratholes.[13]

The reader hardly has to be reminded of the likeness that Solzhenitsyn's description, especially the last paragraph, bears to the collapsing "plaster" and "pasteboard" scenery at the end of *Invitation.*[14]

The flimsy and banal trappings of the fortress in *Invitation* signify the moral decay of this public reality, discredited by the values of conscious life. Literature derives from consciousness and reflects its values. In Nabokov's artifice, therefore, average reality is spontaneously dismantled when Cincinnatus's consciousness confronts the utter lack of human meaning in this world. Because Nabokov does not seek to make his literary artifice appear continuous with natural laws, he can make distinctions that are unavailable to the realist. He does not have to credit average reality, or its approximation, with "real, authentic" reality. Employing the techniques of artifice, he may distinguish between the categories of average and individually true reality. Cincinnatus's ultimate liberation debunks the inferior realm of public reality without purporting to obliterate it in our own lives. Cincinnatus's dramatic plight as a prisoner engages our profound attention without seeking our historical faith. Celebrating the enduring freedoms of consciousness, the artificer abstains from masking his improbable story with the illusion of literal authenticity. Thus *Invitation to a Beheading* is no escapist flight of the imagination. Through artifice, Nabokov truthfully locates the triumphs of human consciousness outside, or beyond, the temporal sphere of historical reality—where tyranny, brute force, and "better guns" will always have a field day.

CHAPTER IV

Putting Two and One Together: *Bend Sinister*

In his introduction to the 1964 American edition of *Bend Sinister*, Nabokov points out the "obvious affinities" between this novel and *Invitation to a Beheading*. The settings of both novels mirror the "idiotic and despicable regimes," the "worlds of tyranny and torture," that have wracked the twentieth century in both revolutionary and reactionary forms of totalitarianism. In *Bend Sinister*, the police state's brutal attempt to inflict its version of "average reality" on the individual's private existence is directed by the dictator Paduk, head of the Party of the Average Man. Paduk presides over "a tyrannic state [which] is at war with its own subjects and may hold any citizen in hostage with no law to restrain it."[1] Like Cincinnatus, Adam Krug, the protagonist of *Bend Sinister*, is a political hostage; but Krug's position is shared by countless other characters in the novel. The new regime is busy making hostages of *all* its citizens, as it strategically encroaches on their individual freedom. Only scattered portions of the population have, as yet, been imprisoned, but the future is grimly predictable.

Despite these obviously political elements, Nabokov insisted that the "story in *Bend Sinister* is not really about life and death in a grotesque police state" (p. xiii). As in *Invitation*, his aim was not primarily to examine and reflect the horrors of a social situation and analyze the historical circumstances which led to it. Once again the techniques of artifice obviate the claims of formal realism, disposing of the illusion of literal authenticity. According to Nabokov, the dictator Paduk, his lackeys, the "farcical policeman Mac," and "the brutal and imbecile soldiers" are not credible characters so much as "absurd mirages, illusions oppressive to Krug during his brief spell of being, but harmlessly fading away when I dismiss the cast" (pp. xiii-xiv).

Reading Nabokov's own description of *Bend Sinister*, one can almost hear the groans of his impatient critics. Immediately following the novel's original publication in 1947, a disappointed critic lamented its artificial ending, which, he said, reduces to irreality the main character's plight: "And when Nabokov himself steps in deliberately at the end, like the puppet-master, and draws up his strings and removes Krug, why then the disillusion is complete. Brilliant, brilliant, but after all it was not real, he was not hurt, we need not be concerned, there is the puppet hanging, and here is the master himself, large as life, smiling at us."[2] The assumption, by now a familiar one, is that by announcing the artifice Nabokov dismisses the reality of his character. But in his introduction to the novel, Nabokov claims that just the opposite holds true. The nature, intensity, and glory of Krug's subjective life are what this novel, with all its elaborate patterning, is primarily *about*: "The main theme of *Bend Sinister*, then, is the beating of Krug's loving heart, the torture an intense tenderness is subjected to" (p. xiv). This is the indestructible reality of human consciousness, which persists and endures in our minds after the "invented habitus" of *Bend Sinister* is dissolved by its creator. As in *Invitation*, the devices of artifice allow Nabokov to render the regime of Paduk and his minions as both malevolently evil and basely unreal. Only in literature, where human meaning is the very source of life, can something so concretely manifest as the Ekwilist state be morally deprived of reality. Subhuman imbecility may spawn brutal and unthinkable deeds, but the secrets of true consciousness will forever elude it. The distinction Nabokov makes between mechanical force and creative power should not lead us to dismiss Krug's suffering or the perverse crimes perpetrated by the inane social machine. Who in the twentieth century is in a position to dismiss the terrible potency of machines— whether bombs or bureaucracies—to unleash random destruction in the refutation of all human meaning and purpose? Krug's suffering and his love, his mental and emotional agony, are as real as anything in literature can be, no matter that Nabokov locates his character's existence in declared artifice. Literary reality, in any case, is confined to the corresponding thoughts or images that develop in the reader's consciousness through the immaterial power of the written word. If Nabokov admits this, uses it to celebrate the glory of his character's conscious life, should we cease to "be concerned" with the significance of Krug's existence in our own minds? No one who calls Krug a puppet would be happy to admit the conclusion that logically follows from such a hasty assumption: fiction, that which by definition has been invented, becomes essentially irrelevant, not serious, because it has not *actually* taken place. In *Bend Sinister*, Nabokov's depiction of the Ekwilist regime is highly fantastical, but truth and seriousness inhere in every aspect of the artifice.

In a world where brute power seeks to extinguish conscious life, the dictator Paduk is aptly nicknamed "the Toad." Bestowed on Paduk by his perceptive boyhood classmates, the nickname has since been outlawed. The old name of the new dictator goes underground—emerging, however, in Krug's subversive mental life and uninhibited conversation. Krug's candid use of the nickname, when referring to the despot, obviously unsettles the president of the university where Krug is a professor of philosophy. Dr. Azureus lamely insists to Krug: "I do not quite follow you, Professor. I do not know who the . . . whom the word or name you used refers to and—what you mean" (p. 49). As the novel develops, we begin to see how Paduk fits into the subhuman species of brute murderer introduced by our discussion of Dreyer's wife, Martha. Martha, we recall, is also perceived as a toad. The evil toad is a popular figure in fairy tales and, as we have observed in both *King, Queen, Knave* and *Invitation to a Beheading*, Nabokov's depiction of subhuman evil breaks the laws of natural appearance with its "fairytale freedom" of approach.

Perhaps this is another reason why Monsieur Pierre, the pragmatic executioner in *Invitation*, argues against fairy tales to Cincinnatus; this vain and perfumed dandy secretly understands the indelicate role he would be assigned in any fairy tale. Stripped of the guise of public concern, Pierre's brutal intentions would be aptly rendered by an ugly toad. In a sense, *Invitation to a Beheading* does prove to be something of a fairy tale: The fortress's external reality is gradually brought into line with the moral decay eating away at appearances. In the end, the plump little executioner Pierre (resembling Gogol's scented emissary of the devil, Pavel Chichikov) is appropriately reduced to the worm he is: "The last to rush past was a woman in a black shawl, carrying the tiny executioner like a larva in her arms" (p. 223).[3]

According to the same kind of expressly literary (and moral) laws, Paduk is depicted as extremely ugly and repulsive. He is so atrociously toadlike that the narrator ironically expresses his desire to beautify Paduk for the sake of credibility. Parodying our expectations for realistic description, however, the author calls for a mortician to do the job properly: "Now the skin is thoroughly cleansed and has assumed a smooth marchpane color. A glossy wig with auburn and blond tresses artistically intermixed covers his head. Pink paint has dealt with the unseemly scar. Indeed, it would be an admirable face, were we able to close his eyes for him. But no matter what pressure we exert upon the lids, they snap open again" (p. 144). Only a hand practiced in dressing up the dead should attempt the beautification of the deathly Paduk; and even then his dummy existence, simulating life in its mechanical functions, resists the completed picture. The eyes intractably pop open. It is difficult to say whether Paduk represents life simulating death or vice versa. Once again we find that Nabokov's self-conscious rendering of Paduk is not just a literary "game," but an attempt to clarify our perception of the human. A dummy is a fake human being, lacking the vital qualities of mind or soul— what we have been calling consciousness, the term favored by Nabokov. Paduk is a dummy because, like Martha, Gradus, and Cincinnatus's jailers, he exists in a soulless condition, hostile to those signs of conscious life which he has forfeited. For the sake of clarity, then, we should reserve the term "puppet" for those Nabokovian creatures who demonstrate the principle of death-in-literary-life, and not mix them up with the numerous characters whom Nabokov endows with the animate qualities of conscious existence.

Paduk's Party of the Average Man holds up the padograph, a machine that simulates human handwriting, "as a proof of the fact that a mechanical device can reproduce personality, and that Quality is merely the distributional aspect of Quantity" (p. 68). Equating quality with quantity, the Ekwilists literally behave and "think" like machines. As a philosopher of international repute, Krug is important to the Ekwilists. They seek his public support for the new university they want to open and, of course, control. Anticipating Krug's useful appearance at the opening ceremonies, the Ekwilists automatically assign the great thinker a ratio of one to their leader's six on the mechanical scale of quantitative significance: "And the one great thinker in the country would appear in scarlet robes (click) beside the chief and symbol of the State (click, click, click, click, click, click) and proclaim in a thundering voice that the State was bigger and wiser than any mortal could be" (p. 153). The clicks signify, of course, that ubiquitous organ of average reality, the newspaper publicity shot.

The "intricate convolutions of sheer stupidity" (p. 112) that set Paduk's world in motion prove a puzzle to Krug, whose philosophical mind is always engaged in the pursuit of meaning. The narrator of the novel also expresses his bafflement. At one point the narrator is obliged to depict a meeting between Krug and Paduk, for Paduk wants Krug to sign a paper affirming the new regime. The meeting of mind and machine poses a literary problem, which the narrator initially solves by treating the encounter as a farce. He reduces the onerous State's functionaries to a comical cast devoid of human reality: "The door opened slightly and a fat gray parrot with a note in its beak walked in. It waddled towards the desk on clumsy hoary legs and its claws made the kind of sound that unmanicured dogs make on varnished floors" (pp. 146-147). Parrots merely simulate human speech, as the padograph simulates human handwriting. Yet this parrot does not even "parrot" the message; he carries it in his beak. The superfluous parrot represents the aimlessness of bureaucratic involution, which the narrator must try to depict. At this point his imagination cannot refrain from gracing Paduk with a touch of spontaneity: "Paduk jumped out of his chair, walked rapidly towards the old bird and kicked it like a football out of the room. Then he shut the door with a bang. The telephone was ringing its heart out on the desk. He disconnected the current and clapped the whole thing into a drawer. And now the answer,' he said" (p. 147). We recognize the narrator's problem: His consciousness goes to work animating the texture of reality with a sense of significance, infusing with life even creatures who are really dummies. As a result, the telephone starts "ringing its heart out" in an office where the mere assertion of human personality is a crime. Exposing the devices of literary artifice, the narrator admits that he has to start over: "No, it did not go on quite like that. In the first place Paduk was silent during most of the interview. What he did say amounted to a few curt platitudes. To be sure, he did do some drumming on the desk (they all drum) and Krug retaliated with some of his own drumming but otherwise neither showed nervousness" (p. 148). The meeting proceeds with "curt platitudes"; the characters' gestures and the narrator's language grow redundant with the monotony of the so-called event. Needless to say, no *real* meeting—in the sense that minds meet—ever takes place: "Paduk curtly asked Krug whether his (Krug's) apartment were warm enough (nobody, of course, could have expected a revolution *without* a shortage of coal), and Krug said yes, it was" (p. 148). The narrator makes witty comments in parenthetical asides, simply to enliven the redundant and pointless conversation. Everything is horribly predictable, like the mechanical "disappearance and reappearance" of the trademark on a rotated pencil: "As [Paduk's] thoughts took a different course, he changed the position of the pencil: he now held it by the ends, horizontally, rolling it slightly between the finger and thumb of either hand, seemingly interested in the disappearance and reappearance of Eberhard Faber No. 2⅜" (p. 149). One imagines the narrator at his own desk, rotating the prototype of Paduk's Eberhard Faber between thumb and forefinger as he ponders the dead end of Paduk's mechanical nature. The colorful meeting that does not take place in the dictator's office remains, nonetheless, imprinted in our minds. The nonexistent parrot illuminates the absurdity of the average reality that Paduk has forged into an iron law of the Average Man.

Literary artifice, which does not assign a position of priority to that which has actually happened, demonstrates how literal or historical events may pale before the reality of meaningful revery. At the opening of *Bend Sinister*, Krug's wife, Olga, has just died, but Krug continues to mourn her throughout the novel. Death excludes Olga from taking part in the plot's chronological order of events; within the literary artifice, however, her death is only technical. As a figment of Krug's memory, imagination, and dreams, Olga "lives" with an intensity denied Paduk and his like:

> As you went the way you had come (now with the palm of your hand open), the sun that had been lying in state on the parquetry of the drawing room and on the flat tiger (spread-eagled and bright-eyed beside the piano), leaped at you, climbed the dingy soft rungs of your jersey and struck you right in the face so that all could see (crowding, tier upon tier, in the sky, jostling one another, pointing, feasting their eyes on the young *radabarbára*) its high color and fiery freckles, and the hot cheeks as red as the hind

wings basally, for the moth was still clinging to your hand . . . (P. 136)

Krug appears to be recalling a moment of past time, but it is a moment he has not personally witnessed. He reconstructs this event in Olga's life from his own memory and the intimate knowledge of his wife's past. All that his memory supplies is the recollection of "a green lane near an orchard and a sturdy young girl carefully carrying a lost fluffy nestling, but whether it had been really [Olga] no amount of probing and poking could either confirm or disprove" (p. 137). Krug, the philosopher, confronts the element of the unknown in his own past, and yet the knowledge kindled by emotion transforms the meager facts into a detailed evocation of the dead woman's own girlhood. Nature pays court to his beloved queen of fifteen years, and the sun rises to celebrate the royal occasion when her life first brushed his in a green lane by an orchard. In the timeless realm of Krug's ardent consciousness, the past fuses with the future, and Olga is envisioned as a child already dead. Like Olga's image, the sun has "been lying in state" until resurrected from apparent death by Krug's loving recollection. The jostling crowds in the sky gaze at the moment from eternity. These images formed by memory, imagination, and the heart expand the bare skeleton of what "happens"; and the ostensible plot proves to be the most finite aspect of Nabokov's fiction.

More than thirty years ago, Diana Trilling reviewed *Bend Sinister* and, like many critics today, expressed distaste and even outrage at being "played" with and manipulated by Nabokov's deliberately self-conscious mode of fiction. She disparaged his "claustrophobic style," which is "wilful" and wields a kind of verbal tyranny over the reader. The reader is "led by meaningless associations into blind alleys and trapped in boredom," and his "mind is allowed to do no work of its own." In her view, Nabokov's style has political ramifications: "The passivity of mind and spirit demanded by *Bend Sinister* is not as far removed as may appear from the passivity of mind and spirit demanded by dictatorial governments, and . . . when we submit ourselves to it we are perhaps betraying a disenchantment with more than old literary methods."[4] For Trilling, Nabokov's difficult prose is more harmful than the aesthete's mere egotism; it is "elaborate chicanery" which masks, apparently, the author's hostility to psychic freedom. As an example of such "chicanery," Trilling cites one of the most resonant passages in *Bend Sinister*.

At the close of the novel's fourth chapter, Krug returns at night from the arranged meeting of the university faculty, where he has refused to sign a statement, prepared by Paduk's officials, declaring his support for the new regime. He finds a young couple kissing on the porch of the building where he lives; they appear to have returned from a costume ball, for he is dressed as an American football player, she as Carmen:

> They separated and he caught a glimpse of her pale, dark-eyed, not very pretty face with its glistening lips as she slipped under his door-holding arm and after one backward glance from the first landing ran upstairs trailing her wrap with all its constellation—

Cepheus and Cassiopeia in their eternal bliss, and the
dazzling tear of Capella, and Polaris the snowflake
on the grizzly fur of the Cub, and the swooning galaxies—those mirrors of infinite space *qui m'effrayent,
Blaise*, as they did you, and where Olga is not, but
where mythology stretches strong circus nets, lest
thought, in its ill-fitting tights, should break its old
neck instead of rebouncing with a hep and a hop—
hopping down again into this urine-soaked dust to
take that short run with the half pirouette in the middle and display the extreme simplicity of heaven in
the acrobat's amphiphorical gesture, the candidly
open hands that start a brief shower of applause
while he walks backwards and then, reverting to
virile manners, catches the little blue handkerchief,
which his muscular flying mate, after her own exertions, takes from her heaving hot bosom—heaving
more than her smile suggests—and tosses to him, so
that he may wipe the palms of his aching weakening
hands. (Pp. 60-61)

A rich cadenza of developed themes and motifs, pre-
paring for what will later unfold, this passage is demonstrably significant in every detail. The intricate
narrative style traces the web of Krug's thoughts and
his simultaneous attempt to quell the emotions of his
private agony. To begin with, the encounter on the
stairs is integral to the novel's plot. The girl dressed as
Carmen foreshadows Mariette, the sluttish young
nursemaid who reminds Krug of a little Carmen.
While she teasingly attracts the unsuspecting father,
Mariette carries out the regime's plans for kidnapping
Krug's child. When Mariette later appears in the
novel to offer her services, Krug has a faint recollection of having seen her before: "Krug had a confused
feeling that he had seen her before, probably on the

stairs. Cinderella, the little slattern, moving and dust-
ing in a dream, always ivory pale and unspeakably
tired after last night's ball" (p. 139). Consistent with
his impression of the kissing Carmen, Mariette strikes
Krug as "not particularly pretty." Mariette's appearance is shrouded in clues that reveal the suspect nature of her mission. She arrives with "good references
from the Department of Public Health," and Krug
mildly accepts them as though he were living in tran-
quil Switzerland instead of a totalitarian regime,
where trusty employees are the State's most ruthless
functionaries. Again, he makes no connection between Mariette's previous employment with "the
well-known artist who lived in apartment 30 right
above Krug" and the more recent departure of that
artist and his wife for "a much less comfortable prison camp in a remote province" (p. 139). The ironic
tone in which the narrator presents these facts suggests that Krug's consciousness has not absorbed
them. They are there, in the pattern, but Krug's perceptions of the girl, detailed and accurate in their own
way, reflect the exclusive preoccupations of his mind
and heart. He recalls the stairs and "last night's ball"
and senses the loss of magic in Mariette's daytime
appearance; yet he cannot make the practical connection. He does not recognize that Mariette, like the
young Carmen on the porch, is in disguise, just as he
consistently fails to detect the most clumsy and crude
stratagems of the regime. The Ekwilists' ludicrous
bumbling ultimately dupes the wise philosopher.

The presence of these obvious clues and the jarring
tone of the narrator's intrusive voice, wryly remarking on the "much less comfortable" accommodations

of the prison camp, are just the thing that Nabokov's hostile critics attack in his literary style. The narrator calls attention to his blatant manipulation of the plot and thus shatters any convincing illusion of the character's lifelike autonomy; the character becomes a mere "puppet" dangling from the author's strings. The most consistent effect of Nabokov's artifice is not, however, to destroy the life of a character, but to track the curve of that character's consciousness, thereby illuminating what consciousness *is* and how it operates. As Nabokov states in his introduction to *Bend Sinister*, *krug* is the Russian word for circle, or circumference (p. xv). In this novel about Krug, Nabokov employs the techniques of artifice to illustrate how his main character selects and forms his perceptions of the world. The world Krug perceives is a psychic landscape, centered around his own preoccupations and concerns. Although Krug has the "confused feeling" that he has seen the young girl before, he cannot identify her. She is a daytime Cinderella, the shadow of her midnight, enchanted self. The magic of that girl was never really hers, as the reader knows, but part of Krug's revery, for which she was the catalyst. When Krug sees Mariette, he fails to metamorphose her into the same enchanted being; without the magic that Krug's consciousness may bestow on her, Mariette appears more like the "slattern" she is than the bewitching Carmen of Krug's imagination.

Everything Krug perceives is transmuted and infused by the grief, the love, the loss he experiences at Olga's death. Within Nabokov's literary artifice, the "pathetic fallacy" is revealed to be a principle of consciousness, and shadows *are* "farewell shadows" for a parting couple and the grieving widower who gazes at them (p. 59). With a sudden stab of recollection, Krug transforms the girl's "spangled wrap" of black gauze into the dark vault of the sky, where the immortal residents of constellations blaze and circle in "eternal bliss." For a brief moment he seeks his dead wife in the metamorphosis; but the "swooning galaxies" that might hold forth eternity's answer to death transmute, as thought takes hold, into the philosopher's problematical "infinite space." Krug's speculative, trained mind cuts off his dream of a mythological heaven, where man used to project his own image and stave off the terror of emptiness.

Image, memory, idea undergo a continual process of association and transformation as Krug's consciousness engages with his surroundings. The dynamics of this process is analogous to that of metamorphosis in nature. As Alfred Appel, Jr., has said, Nabokov's art "records a constant process of *becoming*."[5] In the quoted passage from *Bend Sinister*, Nabokov's language records this process of becoming; Krug's thoughts and feelings take form as mental images, which, in turn, give rise to other forms of perception. As each detail or suggestion is recognized, it alters and adds to the mind's initial perception, culminating in a new view, a possible revelation. As a novelist, Nabokov has been faulted for creating "ways to build a world, not ways to describe one."[6] But critics may simply be missing the point here, seeking confirmation for their own assumptions about reality. What Nabokov's fiction demonstrates is the way that consciousness goes to work *building* the world it perceives. Individual consciousness touches everything and transforms it while transforming itself.

In the passage singled out by Trilling, for example, Krug's mind, working associatively, develops a metaphor for thought as an acrobat in "ill-fitting tights." Thought is always uncomfortable in the world, hampered by the strictures of logic and reason's limited access to the mysterious workings of the universe. Krug's thought, like the acrobat, soars to infinite space, where he must logically discover that "Olga is not." Infinity one boundary, death's governance of this "urine-soaked" planet the other, Krug's thought rebounds from the contemplation of the unknown. He is consoled only by those metaphors which describe and order his dilemma. Krug's mind peoples the unknown as the ancients peopled the heavens. Like the apprehensive audience applauding the acrobat's temporary return to security, he is conscious that thought will have to ascend again to the dizzying heights. The acrobat's "amphiphorical gesture, the candidly open hands" is a graceful flourish that belies the exhaustion and strain those "aching weakening hands" have endured. Thought, however, does not brave the problems of space alone. Near the end of the passage we discover that his "muscular flying mate" has accompanied him all along, undergoing the same strenuous test. Perhaps she is a metaphor for language, or for the associative faculty in consciousness that enables us to perceive analogies, invent metaphors, and verbally order our world. Unannounced until now, "her own exertions," we are told, have cost her "more than her smile [and the artful sentence] suggests." The acrobat's plucky mate may even be an image of Olga's "rosy soul," summoned from the black void by Krug's animating love.[7] Thanks to this able mate, Krug's acrobatic thoughts have not developed in a vacuum. Rather, the philosopher's contemplation of infinity has produced the metaphors that distill meaning from the unknown and rescue him from utter, formless despair. The process by which the kissing couple metamorphose into the acrobat and his loyal little partner both embodies and affirms the mind's salvation from darkness.

As Krug's consciousness makes brave forays into the unknown to ponder the dilemma of existence, events in the plot move irrevocably toward danger and death. Ironically, Krug's intense preoccupation with the ultimate questions of human existence contributes to his personal failure to safeguard his own existence and that of his beloved son, David. He is oblivious to the Ekwilists' spying and the awful logic of their actions. They must find a way to compel Krug's cooperation; eventually, arriving at the obvious, they kidnap David. The gifted thinker is a failure as a detective, missing clue after clue that crops up in the plot. When, for example, two organ-grinders appear in the back yard, under the window of Krug's friend Ember, Krug discerns that something is wrong. "An organ-grinder," he remarks to Ember, "is the very emblem of oneness. But here we have an absurd duality. They do not play but they do glance upwards." The men are suspiciously silent, and Krug notices that outside "the children seem also perplexed by their silence." Ember, with characteristic charm, offers a dramatic interpretation: "And perhaps each is afraid that the other will plunge into some competitive music as soon as one of them starts to play." The upward glance, toward the window at which Krug is standing, hints at the organ-grinders' real business there. Krug, however, is merely amused by what he perceives: "I know of only one other profession that has that upward movement of the eyeballs. And that is our clergy" (p. 124). Both Ember and Krug contribute *their* meaning to the implausible phenomenon, drawing on their own lively perception of the world. Only utter stupidity, however, explains the absurd duality of the organ-grinders, who do not even bother to make music. The bumbling regime has obviously taken a stab at deception, disguising as duplicate organ-grinders the spies they have set on Krug's trail.

The duality of the organ-grinders highlights the corrupt logic of the Ekwilist dogma. According to the regime, quantity is the basic measure of quality; society, art, and even reality are perceived as mere conglomerates. In a recently published memoir, *Hope Against Hope*, Nadezhda Mandelstam, the widow of the Russian poet Osip Mandelstam, describes the system of mass surveillance initiated by Stalin in Russia in the twenties. She recalls how one spy, named "S.," posed as an art lover in order to gain admittance to their coterie of artists and intellectuals:

> S., for instance, first came to us with tales about the East—he said that he was himself originally from Central Asia and had studied in a madrasah there. As proof of his "Eastern" credentials he brought along a small statuette of the Buddha, which could have been bought in any junk store. It was supposed to bear

witness to his expert knowledge of the East and his serious interest in art. The connection between the Buddha and an Islamic madrasah never became clear to us. S. soon lost patience with us and, after making a scene, left us to be taken care of by someone else— or so it appeared, to judge from the equally sudden appearance of another neighbor who also tried to cultivate our acquaintance by bringing us a Buddha! This time it was [Mandelstam] who lost his temper: "Another Buddha! That's enough! They must think of something new!" and he threw out the hapless replacement.[8]

The Stalinists were apparently as blind to the absurdity of dual Buddhas as the Ekwilists to that of dual organ-grinders. In both cases, the casual "oversight" reveals a severe disjunction in perception. By manipulating the elements of artifice, Nabokov reveals more than aesthetic pattern; with a degree of imaginative insight amounting to Solzhenitsyn's "historical comprehension," Nabokov exposes the baffling mental and moral conundrums of the totalitarian mind. For the bureaucrats of a police state, duplication takes the place of originality as a value, and the very notion of authenticity begins to fade from mental view.

Paduk's men attribute no significance to the solitary figure of the organ-grinder, that recurrent "emblem of oneness" in so much Russian and European poetry. Not yet indoctrinated by the Ekwilist dogma, which negates belief in human singularity, the "perplexed" children sense that there is something phony about the silent duo. Krug and Ember, however, do not bother to probe the paradox. Ember invents a theatrical explanation for the organ-grinders' silence;

Krug contemplates the absurd duality without drawing any practical conclusion. Later, when Krug returns to his apartment building, he sees "an organ-grinder of sorts . . . playing *chemin de fer*" with a house detective. Instead of putting two and one together, Krug's mind immediately develops the association between the card game and a railroad, which *chemin de fer* signifies in French. Failing to detect the obvious, Krug nevertheless senses the danger and rapturously envisions a railway car leading out of this terrible world: "And following it along the darkling swamps, and hanging faithfully in the evening aether, and slipping through the telegraph wires, as chaste as a wove-paper watermark, as smoothly moving as the transparent tangle of cells that floats athwart an overworked eye, the lemon-pale double of the lamp that shone above the passenger would mysteriously travel across the turquoise landscape in the window" (pp. 184-185). As the allusions to the "wove-paper watermark" and the author's "overworked eye" suggest, Krug's dream of escaping his world is linked with the author's more fortunate sphere of existence. The reflected lamp Krug envisions is itself a reflection of the one in his creator's room, and consciousness.

The metaphorical railway car, emerging from the train of associations in Krug's mind, does not take him out of his world for more than an instant. But in that instant of supreme consciousness, Krug engages the origins of his existence and makes contact with the world of his creator. Significantly, it is at this moment of profound contact with ultimate reality that Krug proves so disastrously unaware of the regime's machinations. He fails to observe the ludicrous presence of yet another organ-grinder. Commenting on Krug's fatal blindness, Frank Kermode has called him a "tragic Shandy, whose obsessions with intellect, the habit of expecting matters to fall out in accordance with intelligent prediction bring disaster to his son." Yet Kermode sensibly qualifies his comparison, noting the basic difference between the worlds of *Bend Sinister* and *Tristram Shandy*: "The difference between Sterne's comedy and Nabokov's tragedy is simply that the hard facts upon which the Shandys bruise themselves are orderly and to be respected; whereas Krug's victors are aimless and banal, and their policy the corruption of a philosophy."[9] According to Nabokov's arrangement of the "facts," Krug's blindness partly arises from the subhuman nature of the Ekwilists' organization of average reality. Their "intricate convolutions of sheer stupidity" simply elude an intelligence as profound as Adam Krug's.

Nabokov viewed the collective reality of *Bend Sinister* as a "meaningless world" where logic and truth have been supplanted by a "dim-brained brutality which thwarts its own purpose" (introduction, p. xiv). It is "a morally inverted world" where, as Stanley Hyman said, Krug's moral and intellectual strengths turn out to be tactical weaknesses. Krug's "intellectual pride . . . makes him unable to take the dictator and his popular support seriously. The philosophical complexity of his mind leads him to hesitate and delay, so that he does not escape the country when he could . . . And his consuming love for David, now that his wife is dead, is his ultimate vulnerability."[10] Placing Krug's weakness in the proper perspective, then, Nabokov employs artifice to discredit the essential reality of Paduk and his minions while demonstrating their destructive power. Devoid of human significance, the Ekwilists seek to exterminate those who contain within them the capacity to create and to perceive human meaning on earth. What Robert Alter observes of *Invitation to a Beheading* may be profitably applied to *Bend Sinister* as well: "If consciousness is the medium through which reality comes into being, the sudden and final obliteration of consciousness through mechanical means is the supreme affirmation by human agents—the executioners—of the principle of irreality."[11] The Ekwilists do not possess what they seek to destroy; and as agents of human destruction they cannot claim the same degree of reality as their victims.

Nabokov's techniques for granting (literary) life only to those who exhibit its true signs arise from the special logic and truth of his private worlds. Moreover, he adjusts the effects of artifice so that each of the two novels, *Invitation to a Beheading* and *Bend Sinister*, illuminates a different aspect of the relationship between the true reality of unique perception and the average reality of collective existence. Cincinnatus, on the one hand, overestimates the nature and power of his prison environment and its claims to true reality. He bestows too much of his own imaginative talent on a sham world essentially hostile to his radiant conscious life. Thus he comes dangerously close to animating a dead world, devoid of particular meaning and personal values. Misapplying the magic of his creative perception, Cincinnatus nearly brings the parody to life and power. From this Nabokovian perspective, we might suggest that those who take too seriously and too much to heart the current issues and ideological slogans that plague an era—sacrificing their rare and special energies (and their lives) to the general and sometimes mad social machine—may invite their own kind of beheading. They may destroy the possibilities for a classless, unclassifiable, wholly unique experience of life itself. Fanatics who have inflicted mental castration on themselves are the very ones most anxious to assemble the executioner's platform for the rest of us.

In *Bend Sinister*, the main character's plight is somewhat the reverse of Cincinnatus's in *Invitation*. Solely preoccupied with his radiant inner life and the pursuit of ultimate meaning, Adam Krug does not *sufficiently* imagine the characters around him. He does not perceive the lengths to which brutal and ambitious "dummies" will go to implement their ludicrous and detestable notions. Nabokov does not grant human stature to this inhuman kind, but *Bend Sinister* illustrates the dire threat it poses to all humanity—those of us who have in common our uniqueness. To preserve our right to live and perceive as individuals, we must recognize the savagery that attends the forfeiture of human consciousness. (Calibans are far more dangerous to human life than the most savage wild beasts. One reason Nabokov came to write *Bend Sinister* in English is that he removed himself and his family from the clutches of ideological Calibans overrunning a whole continent.) Krug does not seize the chance to escape Paduk's regime with his son, and so the extraordinary philosopher unwittingly condescends to be the dummy of the sub-human dummies he cannot take seriously.

"If you shun consciousness as if it were a plague," Irving Howe wrote some years ago, "then a predicament may ravage you but you cannot cope with it." Unlike Nabokov's use of the term, Howe's reference is, quite explicitly, to social consciousness. His analysis of the relationship between "mass society and post-modern fiction" has had a great influence, it seems, on the way we think about novels today. The problem of contemporary writers, says Howe, is one of establishing the convincing identity of their characters. That identity, like our own, depends on a relationship to the "world of practical affairs"—though, admittedly, the "post-modern" world does not supply much in the way of coherent social orders. The unfortunate result, in Howe's view, is that the characters of some of the finest postwar novels lack "social definition," are oftentimes mere creatures "of literary or even ideological fiat."[12] While sympathetic to contemporary novelists hampered by the lack of social order characterizing "mass society," Howe's insight does not alter his critical judgments:

> Some of the best postwar novels, like *Invisible Man* and *The Adventures of Augie March*, are deeply concerned with the fate of freedom in a mass society; but the assertiveness of idea and vanity of style which creeps into such books are the result, I think, of willing a subject onto a novel rather than allowing it to grow out of a sure sense of a particular moment and place. These novels merit admiration for defending the uniqueness of man's life, but they suffer from having to improvise the terms of this uniqueness. It is a difficulty that seems, at the moment, unavoidable

> . . . Still, it had better be said that the proclamation
> of personal identity in recent American fiction tends,
> if I may use a fashionable phrase, to be more a pro-
> duct of will than of the imagination.[13]

Nabokov's critics still point to the "vanity" of his
elaborate prose style and the "assertiveness" of his
approach to writing novels. The "fiat" by which he
introduces and removes his characters has, as I have
said, irritated countless critics and reviewers. Using
Howe's terms, one could easily regard *Bend Sinister*
as a novel defending "the uniqueness of man's life"
but sadly "improvising" the terms of this uniqueness.
By "improvise," Howe apparently means that the
character's identity is not established through his relationship with society and a "world of practical affairs."

At the same time that Howe restricts the terms of
character depiction within the novel, he does not dis-
own the pernicious dangers of contemporary "mass
society." He entertains the possibility "that we are
moving toward a quiet desert of moderation where
men will forget the passion of moral and spiritual
restlessness that has characterized society. That the
human creature, no longer a Quixote or a Faust, will
become a docile attendant to an automated civiliza-
tion. That the 'aura of the human' will be replaced by
the nihilism of satiety. That the main question will no
longer be the conditions of existence but existence itself."[14] Apparently, for Howe, man's consciousness
rests entirely with the social order. If that order de-
generates, so does the individual's identity. The
bonds of the social organism prove stronger than the
umbilical cord; in this case, the novel, too, must die.

In the fictional mass society where Krug dwells, an engagement with social forces does not define but obliterates the individual's identity. Social consciousness, at some periods of history at least, becomes the enemy of human consciousness. This is the situation reflected in the world of *Bend Sinister*. Here Nabokov affirms that the essential source of human identity is mind, not material; the individual, not society; consciousness, not social consciousness. No matter how stagnant and horrifying the collective life, the individual has the capacity to liberate himself from the tyranny "of a particular moment and place," in order to affirm his own identity and the freedoms of conscious life. Although the savagery and stupidity of Paduk's regime is brilliantly exposed in *Bend Sinister*, Nabokov is primarily concerned with the private sphere of his character's fate, persisting beyond what Erich Auerbach called the "inner processes of the real, historical world."[15] Nabokov's focus is always the inner processes of consciousness and the eternity with which it puts us in touch. The dynamics is not that of historical process shaping character, but of consciousness itself forming reality. No matter what Paduk's regime does to torture Krug, it cannot extinguish the light of his consciousness.

Consciousness is the most indestructible element of human existence, and only Krug's creator has the power to divest him of this essential gift. Taking pity on his character near the end of the novel (Krug's child is mistakenly butchered by the heavy-handed and muddle-headed Ekwilists), the author grants Krug "blessed madness" by exposing him to the origins of his creation. Nabokov describes Krug's revelation: "He suddenly perceives the simple reality of things and knows but cannot express in the words of his world that he and his son and his wife and everybody else are merely my whims and megrims" (introduction, p. xiv). The manifest reality of *Bend Sinister* suddenly pales as Krug glimpses a world beyond its finite borders. Just before "another and better bullet" hits him, he confronts his author, shouting, "You, you—"(p. 240). Divested of apparent mortality, Krug returns "unto the bosom of his maker" (p. xviii).

Like the ancestral Adam in the story of Genesis, Adam Krug acquires knowledge of his universe that expels him from his first world. But while Adam "fell" from eternity to our mortal condition, Krug is figuratively graced with immortality by his creator, though the latter admits that the gift is only a literary trick: "I knew that the immortality I had conferred on the poor fellow was a slippery sophism, a play upon words" (p. 241). The author, like Humbert Humbert, has "only words to play with"; but in literature, at least, death is always "a question of style" (p. 241). A character's death is inevitably artistic, "a mere literary device, a musical resolution" to the verbal composition (p. xviii).

Krug dies by the same literary "fiat" that gave him life. The experience of his resplendently conscious existence endures, however, long after the circle is completed, the book closed. Krug proves "immortal" because, as a literary image, he continues to exist in our minds after his preordained death. His soul leaves its "imprint . . . in the intimate texture of space" artfully arranged by his creator (p. 242). The rule of art, Nabokov suggests, may also reflect a principle of life;

our own death may prove "a question of style," and new terms of existence may supplant previous ones. When, at the end of the novel, the author extinguishes the flame of Krug's "earthly" life, the elements of the apparent universe also fade and dissolve. Like the prison officials in *Invitation to a Beheading*, Paduk the Toad helplessly perishes: Krug "saw the Toad crouching at the foot of the wall, shaking, dissolving, speeding up his shrill incantations, protecting his dimming face with his transparent arm" (p. 240). The world of *Bend Sinister* is dispelled like the trappings of Cincinnatus's fortress, and the "anthropomorphic deity" who has created it recalls us to the "comparative paradise" of his room.

The techniques of self-declared artifice prevent us from identifying with Adam Krug and his world; we have no illusions that such an "invented habitus" is continuous with our own reality. Instead, we share the author's superior vantage point, and are grateful to exist beyond the confines of his created universe. While sharing the author's godlike superiority to his artifice, however, we recognize that within the confines of our own universe our position is analogous to Adam Krug's. Krug is a "galley slave," confined to literary status in a world of words. But we, too, exist within the boundaries of a world largely made up of words. Our universe, as Nabokov said, is a universe "embraced by consciousness." Our limited ability to name, describe, and thereby order our world establishes its character and dimensions. The origins of our existence are ultimately mysterious, remaining beyond the reach of the words we summon to define and describe. Hedged by the unknown surrounding us, we struggle, like Adam Krug, to peer beyond the limits of our condition, seeking to populate the terrifyingly empty spaces with our words and images. We ought not to resent, then, the acrobatic author for summoning lucid metaphors out of the dark; we ought not to be disillusioned when the daring performer acknowledges the limits of his flight while affirming, at the same time, the vast reaches he has scanned. Far from being, as some critics suggest, Nabokov's "clowns" or the opponents he seeks to attack and defeat through clever manipulation, Nabokov's readers are privileged participants in his "game of worlds." Through artifice we are made privy to the secrets of his created universe; and unlike Krug, we may enjoy them at no expense of life or sanity.

CHAPTER V

Singularity and the Double's Pale Ghost: From *Despair* to *Pale Fire*

Despite Nabokov's consistent emphasis on the individual nature of reality and his obvious hostility to the notion of duality, his novels have given rise to innumerable speculations concerning the *Doppelgänger* motif.[1] To mention only a partial list of the many suggested doubles in Nabokov's fiction, there are Hermann and Felix in *Despair*, Albinus and Rex in *Laughter in the Dark*, Cincinnatus and Pierre in *Invitation to a Beheading*, Humbert and Quilty in *Lolita*, Kinbote and Shade in *Pale Fire*, as well as Van and Ada in *Ada*. Evidently exasperated by his critics' preoccupation with the double, Nabokov once dismissed the whole subject as irrelevant. "The *Doppelgänger* subject is a frightful bore." He then added, "There are no 'real' doubles in my novels."[2] Nabokov's distinction here, between "real" doubles and their implied opposite—false or "unreal" doubles—introduces, once again, fundamental issues concerning the nature of the reality depicted in his artifice.

Clarifying certain questions regarding Nabokov's treatment of the double should help us, therefore, to clarify some of the larger issues we have been examining.

Rather than focus this chapter on a single novel, I shall take up several, including *Lolita* and *Pale Fire*, which most often provoke critical discussion of the double in Nabokov's fiction. The first and most obvious is, of course, *Despair*, which was first published serially in 1934. Here we find a solipsistic madman Hermann, the narrator of the novel, who persists in "seeing double." Hermann discovers a wandering tramp named Felix, who appears, in Hermann's eyes, to be his mirror image. Significantly, the subjective nature of Hermann's perception is stated at the very outset. In Hermann's words, Felix "appeared *to my eyes* as my double, that is, as a creature bodily identical with me. It was this absolute sameness which gave me so piercing a thrill."[3] Hermann's discovery later inspires him to proclaim his ideological commitment to such "sameness." His statement also suggests that Hermann's fascination with "sameness" may have contributed to the delusion itself:

> It even seems to me sometimes that my basic theme, the resemblance between two persons, has a profound allegorical meaning. This remarkable physical likeness probably appealed to me (subconsciously!) as the promise of that ideal sameness which is to unite people in the classless society of the future; and by striving to make use of an isolated case, I was, though still blind to social truths, fulfilling nevertheless, a certain social function . . . In fancy, I visualize a new world, where all men will resemble one another as Hermann and Felix did; a world of Helixes

and Fermanns; a world where the worker fallen dead
at the feet of his machine will be at once replaced by
his perfect double smiling the serene smile of perfect
socialism. (Pp. 168-169)

Hermann's version of "perfect socialism" aligns him
with the Ekwilists in *Bend Sinister*, who are eager to
make humanity over in their own mechanical image.
On Felix, his assumed "double," rich and "well-fed"
Hermann acts out his theoretical attraction to (but
ultimate contempt for) the "common man," in this
case a destitute tramp. His enchantment with the notion of human duplication lends itself, like Ekwilism,
to the justification of human annihilation: Hermann
decides to make use of his double by destroying him;
he will then dress Felix's corpse in his own clothes and
collect the considerable life insurance. In light of the
murderer's savage exploitation of his victim, the
"profound allegorical meaning" Hermann reads into
his story is doubly absurd.

The dubious and pernicious logic of Hermann's
claims has, strangely enough, tended to go unrecognized by most critics of the novel. Apparently misled
by the madman's own delusions, they take seriously
his banal identification between the "perfect" murder
he plans to commit and the perfection of a work of
art.[4] While, from the very first page of the novel,
Hermann persists in comparing himself to a poet or
an actor and the staging of the murder to art, Nabokov is hardly suggesting that artistic pretensions
alone make an artist. In the foreword to his revised
English translation of the novel, the author defines
Hermann more directly; he is a "neurotic scoundrel,"
whose sincerity, at least, ought to be questioned (p.

9). Hermann himself tells the reader that he lies "ecstatically," and there is plenty of evidence in the text to support that admission. Claiming, for example, that "there is not a thing about [literature] that I do not know," Hermann repeatedly disproves his own case. When prompted to render "in his own words" the plot of *Othello*, a play "perfectly familiar" to him, he perversely makes "the Moor skeptical and Desdemona unfaithful" (pp. 55-56).[5] As he distorts the plot, characters, and dramatic focus of Shakespeare's tragedy, Hermann distorts, to the shape of his own obsession, whatever else impinges on his consciousness. When his grandiose professions of literary genius are consistently undercut by evidence in the text, how can we allow Hermann's dubious comparison between the murderer and the creative artist to go unchallenged?

From the opening paragraph of the novel, Nabokov invites the reader to examine Hermann's aesthetic posturing not as allegorical truth but as evidence of a deranged psyche. Hermann's ready dismissal of "the law which makes such a fuss over a little spilled blood" should alone alert us to the destructive, rather than creative, impulses at work in his mad mind. In this paragraph, as in every other statement Hermann utters, his mental confusion is betrayed in the style of his argument:

> If I were not perfectly sure of my power to write and of my marvelous ability to express ideas with the utmost grace and vividness . . . So, more or less, I had thought of beginning my tale. Further, I should have drawn the reader's attention to the fact that had I lacked that power, that ability, et cetera, not only

should I have refrained from describing certain recent events, but there would have been nothing to describe, for, gentle reader, nothing at all would have happened. Silly perhaps, but at least clear. The gift of penetrating life's devices, an innate disposition toward the constant exercise of the creative faculty could alone have enabled me . . . At this point I should have compared the breaker of the law which makes such a fuss over a little spilled blood, with a poet or a stage performer.[6]

While declaring the "grace" and "vividness" of his style, the narrator obviously lacks both to an extreme degree, as he struggles to devise a suitable opening for his story. The initial sentence is not really a sentence at all, but a conditional clause, inconclusively left hanging—the aborted form already contradicting the narrator's contention. (The two ellipses in this quotation have been placed here by Nabokov to indicate breaks in Hermann's thought.) Lumpish and uncertain phrases like "more or less" and "et cetera" reveal the essential insecurity behind Hermann's bold assertions of competence. He launches the second paragraph much more defensively: "It may look as though I do not know how to start." Next he apologizes for his "bulky imagery," and in one of the following paragraphs he jerkily disavows the "deliberate lie" he has let slip in the paragraph preceding (pp. 13-14). Frequently writing himself into a corner, Hermann just as often resorts to awkward conversational ploys—"Well, as I was saying"—to get him back on the elusive track. When a new circumstance strikes him as necessary to relate, he interrupts the narrative to add, "I think I ought to inform the reader that there has just been a long interval" (p. 15). Quite obviously, *Despair* is a flamboyant exercise in first-person confessional narrative by Nabokov—his exploitation of the conventions, and weaknesses, of the form. Hermann is the narrator but Nabokov is the artist, who seeks to reveal the obvious limitations of his narrator without unduly punishing the reader. Hermann's pretensions to artistry prompt him, at one point, to fabricate a literary childhood for himself. He claims to have composed "abstruse verse and elaborate stories" as a boy; the claim is followed up by the unwitting admission that he "did not write down those stories" (p. 55). No true writer, of course, would overlook this essential distinction between written and unwritten stories. With similar naïveté Hermann later compares his "masterpiece," the murder, to "a beautiful book [that] is not in the least impaired by a misprint or a slip of the pen" (p. 202). Anyone acquainted with Nabokov's exacting requirements for art will recognize this, at the very least, as a revelation of Hermann's artistic ignorance.

Hermann's only true literary status derives from his function as the narrating persona of *Despair*, the "substitute" author of the novel. Frequent allusions to the conventions of "novels where the narrative is conducted in the first person by the real or substitute author" should remind us that the illusory spontaneity of such confessions is really a device of artifice; in a novel of confession the "first person is as fictitious as all the rest" (p. 53). Frequently burlesquing the breathless, urgent immediacy of Dostoevsky's confessional narrators, Nabokov also parodies the elevated tone of Raskolnikov's metaphysical conflict—to mur-

der or not to murder—in *Crime and Punishment*. As
many readers have noted, Hermann frequently compares himself to Raskolnikov; alluding to "Dusty," he
even considers *Crime and Pun* and *Crime and Slime*
as possible titles for his tale.

Dostoevsky's use of murder as a philosophical
paradigm is, for Nabokov, an absurdity.[7] As he demonstrates so thoroughly in *King, Queen, Knave,*
murder is always banal and derivative—a lethal form
of meaninglessness like the Ekwilists' "convolutions
of sheer stupidity" in *Bend Sinister*. Considering the
context of *Despair* and Nabokov's other fiction, I
cannot see how Hermann's delusions are meant to
shed any light whatsoever on the real practice or perfection of art. In Nabokov's view, only those who are
mentally deficient, like Hermann, or fatally misguided would mistake the brutal act of murder for an
illumination of the mysteries of artistic creation. Hermann's "perfect" crime is, in fact, a consummate bun-
gle. At the end of the novel, with a sudden cry of recognition, Hermann moans, "What on earth have I
done?" (p. 220). This is, in Nabokov's words, the
"sonorous howl" of true despair which breaks
through Hermann's ecstatic lies and fantasies (foreword, p. 7). In Raskolnikov's case, Dostoevsky suggests that there may be a redeeming value to his
crime. Thus Porfiry Petrovich says to Raskolnikov,
"Seek and ye shall find. Perhaps God was even awaiting you in this," Raskolnikov's crime.[8] Nabokov dis-
dained such theoretical (or theological) justifications
for brutality, avowing that "Hell shall never parole
Hermann" (foreword, p. 9). Hermann's final gesture
of despair is itself a mockery of sophistic attempts to

qualify and justify murder: "Let us suppose, I kill an
ape. Nobody touches me. Suppose it is a particularly
clever ape. Nobody touches me. Suppose it is a new
ape—a hairless, speaking species. Nobody touches
me. By ascending these subtle steps circumspectly, I
may climb up to Leibnitz or Shakespeare and kill
them, and nobody will touch me, as it is impossible
to say where the border was crossed, beyond which
the sophist gets into trouble" (p. 177).

Nabokov's parody of Dostoevsky's "sensitive murderers" also draws on Dostoevsky's fondness for
creating Romantic doubles in his fiction. In *Crime
and Punishment*, for example, Svidrigaylov mysteriously appears before Raskolnikov on various occa-
sions and like an evil alter ego reads the young man's
most hidden thoughts. An amoral "breaker of the
law" (to quote Hermann), Svidrigaylov suggests that
he and Raskolnikov are "berries from the same field,"
or as we say in English, birds of a feather.[9] In *Despair*, however, the *Doppelgänger* motif becomes a
deceptive shadow-theme, tracing the delusions of
Hermann's mad mind. The ultimate effect of the parody is to throw into bold relief the singular nature of
human identity. Ardalion, a painter (and the lover of
Hermann's wife) objects to Hermann's obsession with
resemblance and the "types" of human faces. Declaring to Hermann that "every face is unique," Ardalion
develops his argument: "You'll say next that all
Chinamen are alike. You forget, my good man, that
what the artist perceives is, primarily, the *difference*
between things. It is the vulgar who note their resemblance" (p. 51). Ardalion's own vulgar expression
notwithstanding, his argument is persuasive. (In the

Russian original, he says "Japanese" rather than "Chinamen"; *Otchaianie*, p. 41.) As it turns out, the resemblance between Hermann and his victim is only the projection of a mind obsessed with "sameness." No one but Hermann detects the slightest resemblance between the murderer and his supposed "double." Hermann is shocked and outraged that Felix's unique identity is taken for granted by others. The police not only fail to observe any resemblance, Hermann tells us, they also express "surprise at my having hoped to deceive the world simply by dressing up in my clothes an individual who was not in the least like me." Hermann comments, "The next logical step was to make me mentally deficient; they even went so far as to suppose I was not quite sane and certain persons knowing me confirmed this" (p. 201).

In Nabokov's fiction, it is only the Ekwilists or madmen who believe in human "doubles," those duplicates of the self. In *Bend Sinister*, the philosopher Adam Krug recognizes, nevertheless, a kind of psychic rift in his own consciousness, which he calls the "last stronghold" of abhorrent dualism. When Krug learns, at the opening of the novel, that his wife's operation has not been successful and that she will die, he experiences the sensation of being two people: "As usual he discriminated between the throbbing one and the one that looked on: looked on with concern, with sympathy, with a sigh, or with bland surprise. This was the last stronghold of the dualism he abhorred. The square root of I is I" (p. 6). Krug distinguishes, then, between that aspect of his consciousness which succumbs to the overwhelming circumstances of the moment and his innermost self, able to withstand the chaotic onslaught of emotion. The latter self is the conscious observer, who does not wholly identify with the transitory pain and pleasure flooding a particular instant. Franz, in *King, Queen, Knave*, demonstrably lacks this aspect of consciousness; he is continually overwhelmed, and victimized, by immediate sensation. Krug, on the other hand, pictures this aspect of his self as a "stranger quietly watching the torrents of local grief from an abstract bank": "He saw me crying when I was ten and led me to a looking glass in an unused room . . . so that I might study my dissolving face. He has listened to me with raised eyebrows when I said things which I had no business to say. In every mask I tried on, there were slits for his eyes" (p. 6). There is something in human beings more stable than personality and the social masks we assume in public, something more lasting than the fleeting impulses and wayward reactions that bind us to the moment and imprison us in time. The enduring self that learns, watches, and grows from experience—this is the self that stores an image from the present in order to recall it in the future. At a moment of intense and potentially overwhelming grief, Krug regards this essential self as his "savior," his "witness" (p. 6).[10]

The experience of duality is shown, in so much of Nabokov's fiction, to be an aberration of consciousness or the symptom of a psyche in distress. There are "no 'real' doubles" in Nabokov's novels because "seeing double" is only, as in Hermann's case, the reflection of one man's obsession with resemblance. In *Lolita*, for example, Humbert's identification with Clare Quilty, frequently alleged to be his double or alter ego, is really an expression of his own self-loathing. Quilty's depravity presents an obvious mirror for Humbert's tormented conscience. As he tussles on the floor with the man he is about to kill, Humbert literally confuses Quilty's identity with his own: "He was naked and goatish under his robe, and I felt suffocated as he rolled over me. I rolled over him. We rolled over me. They rolled over him. We rolled over us."[11] It may well be true that in killing Quilty Humbert seeks to kill himself, or that part of himself he hates, but to go along with Humbert's desperate act of projection here is to succumb to the kind of pernicious logic evinced by mad Hermann. Once we assume, as Martin Green does, that by killing Quilty Humbert "purge[s] himself symbolically," we have managed to abstract from reality the horror of the act itself. Like Hermann's destruction of his "double," Humbert's murder of Quilty is symbolically interpreted—as a paradigm for the process of art. Specific reality is boiled down to "synthetic jam"; and murder is dubiously regarded as both necessary and laudable. Green writes: "Art can confer immortality, of a consciously limited and conditional kind, . . . and therefore art is glorious, in all its artificiality and trickery. The artist is a kind of hero. Humbert killed Quilty because [here Green quotes from the novel] 'One had to choose between him and H. H., and one wanted H. H. to exist at least a couple of months longer so as to have him make you [Lolita] live in the minds of later generations.' "[12]

No matter what symbolic construction is placed on the act of murder, to regard Humbert as a "hero" for murdering Quilty seems a dreadful misconception of

both Nabokov's intentions and the moral fabric of
the novel. In my opinion, the *only* artist justified in
killing off Quilty for the sake of art (and the artful
narration) is his creator, Nabokov. The author of the
artifice reserves the right to dictate the course of
events in the private world of his creation. *Within* the
fictional framework, however, the murder of one
character by another may not be so lightly dismissed.
The murderer's peculiar relationship to his victim, a
relationship explored by Nabokov in many of the
novels we have already discussed, is an essential the-
matic element in *Lolita* as well. Allegorical explanations only serve to obscure the moral and psychological issues with which Humbert himself has to grap-
ple.[13]

Seeking to discharge his "load of revenge" through
Quilty's heart, Humbert fatally pulls the trigger, but
as he points out, his plan for revenge backfires: "Far
from feeling any relief, a burden even weightier than
the one I had hoped to get rid of was with me, upon
me, over me. I could not bring myself to touch him in
order to make sure he was really dead" (p. 306). His
description contains verbal echoes—"with me, upon
me, over me"—recalling Humbert's earlier tumble
with Quilty and the resulting confusion, or coupling,
of their identities in Humbert's mind. Now, however,
the physical weight of Quilty's body is to be replaced
by the "even weightier" psychic burden of his corpse.
Murder has neither purged Humbert of his guilt nor
rid him of his obsession. Leaving Pavor Manor with a
"heavy heart," Humbert continues to feel "all covered
with Quilty" (pp. 307-308). It is with this sense of being "all covered with Quilty" that Humbert narrates

the novel; and it accounts for Quilty's uncanny "shadowing" of Humbert and Lolita in their cross-country trek. As Humbert describes the mystery man's unnatural success in the nightmarish pursuit (aided by Lolita's clandestine assistance), the eerie shadow begins to take on the attributes of a supernaturally able detective. "Quilty is so ubiquitous," says Alfred Appel, Jr., "because he formulates Humbert's entrapment, his criminal passion, his sense of shame and self-hate."[14] Quilty is also ubiquitous because, within the frame of fictional events, Humbert has killed the pursuer *long before* he recounts this cross-country pursuit. When introducing Quilty's red convertible into his narrative for the first time, Humbert simultaneously reminds us that he is "a murderer with a sensational but incomplete and unorthodox memory" (p. 219). Thus we should realize that the increasingly supernatural appurtenances of the "red ghost" in Humbert's rear-view mirror emanate from the ghostly power of Quilty's apparition within the murderer's "sensational" memory. The "blood" and "bits of marrow sticking to" Humbert's "story" are the ghastly remains that the murderer cannot mentally shake off (p. 310).

By murdering Quilty, the "semi-animated, subhuman trickster" he despises, Humbert perceives, paradoxically, that he has "disregarded all laws of humanity" (pp. 297, 308). If, as Charles Kinbote says, the murderer is always inferior to his victim, then what status may poor Humbert claim, having slain the "subhuman" monster? Throughout *Lolita*, Humbert cannot forget that he is, indeed, a murderer, and that Quilty's death as well as Lolita's lost childhood are on his conscience. Repeatedly, and from the novel's first page, he derisively sabotages his own efforts to confess, to explain, to exonerate himself in some way. He thus warns the reader, "You can always count on a murderer for a fancy prose style" (p. 11). The patterns of *Lolita* have psychological as well as aesthetic significance, and Humbert's language is more than a virtuoso display of effects: it is a strong but delicate instrument that registers the slightest, as well as the wildest, oscillations of Humbert's distressed mind and heart. Humbert's language, like Hermann's in *Despair*, reveals what he cannot say directly.

The self-conscious design of *Lolita*, fabricated from so much parody and allusion, is obviously responsible, to some degree, for the tendency of critics to interpret the novel's action symbolically. As I have tried to show, Nabokov's elaborate artifice has similarly prompted critics to discount or ignore the reality of his characters. Many commentators on *Pale Fire*, for example, have been so struck by the novel's intricate patterns and overlapping spheres of perception that they assign to either Kinbote or Shade the authorship of the whole novel. Implicitly faithful to the traditional assumption that pattern and artifice constrict a character's possibilities for literary life, such critics appear to seek some redeeming authenticity, outside the artifice, for one of *Pale Fire*'s two central characters. When three-dimensional reality is claimed for either Shade or Kinbote, the other is demoted to the status of the "real" character's double, or projected self. Thus Kinbote is assigned the role of John Shade's dark alter ego, or else Shade is seen as a pale reflection of the more brilliant Kinbote.[15] Some critics seek authenticity in the artifice by treating the characters as Nabokov's own doubles or "equivalents."[16] But if, despite Nabokov's protestations, we decide that one of his characters is the other's double, or the author's own, we may find ourselves preoccupied, like mad Hermann, with unlikely resemblances where Nabokov has sought to evoke individual reality and unique differences.

In *Pale Fire*, Charles Kinbote's alleged intimacy with John Shade is, after all, only an illusion. Although he is fascinated by the poet, and even more so by Shade's poem, Kinbote is basically indifferent to Shade as an individual. And even though Kinbote does not do violence to Shade physically, his delusions are frequently as destructive in nature as those of Hermann. The man who narcissistically perceives others only as reflections of himself is bound to prove indifferent to their fate as unique beings. Thus we find Kinbote, one lonely spring, wishing that Shade would have a heart attack, just to break the monotony of Kinbote's own solitude: "What would I not have given for the poet's suffering another heart attack . . . leading to my being called over to their house, all windows ablaze, in the middle of the night, in a great warm burst of sympathy, coffee, telephone calls, Zemblan herbal receipts (they work wonders!), and a resurrected Shade weeping in my arms."[17] In his melodramatic fantasy, Kinbote plays the part of tender healer; but through the self-flattery the ironies emerge. Kinbote dreamily supposes that wonder-working "herbal receipts" would aid the victim of a heart attack—a heart attack that the tender Hippocrates of this little drama has actually wished upon the patient! After Shade is successfully shot through the heart by a mad assassin, Kinbote abandons the poet's body, lying face down on the ground, and rushes into the Goldsworths' house to hide the dead man's manuscript. Although Kinbote has already noted the "red spot on [Shade's] white shirt," he expresses the vague hope that Shade "had not been killed"; needless to say, he does not pause in his flight to the house to find out. After securing the "treasure," the poem *Pale Fire*, in a closet, Kinbote returns, absurdly, "with a glass of water" (pp. 294-295). Will it, too, "work wonders" for the murdered man, who has been shot while humanely attempting to draw Kinbote out of the line of fire? Even as a corpse, kindly John Shade reminds us of that bright internal world of sympathy and love which is largely unavailable to his mad amanuensis.

In contrast to Shade's heartiness, Kinbote's misery produces in him a vaguely expressed fascination with "beautiful" death. "If I were a poet," he says, "I would certainly make an ode to the sweet urge to close one's eyes and surrender utterly unto the perfect safety of wooed death. Ecstatically one forefeels the vastness of the Divine Embrace enfolding one's liberated spirit, the warm bath of physical dissolution, the universal unknown engulfing the minuscule unknown that had been the only real part of one's temporary personality" (p. 221). He later adds, "We who burrow in filth every day may be forgiven perhaps the one sin that ends all sins" (p. 222). Kinbote's fascination with suicide is also revealed in the Index to his Commentary, where he describes Hazel Shade as "having preferred the beauty of death to the ugliness of life" (p. 312). Only in his dreams and his wildest Zemblan fancies does mad Kinbote manage to transmute the "drab prose" of his unhappy existence into "strong and strange poetry" (p. 209). Beneath the stylistic bravado and ostentatious conceit lurk awful doubts and the shadowy fear of persecution, punctuated by unbearable headaches and Kinbote's recurrent impulse to slip through his daily torment into a "warm bath of physical dissolution." Meanwhile, before such "release" is granted Kinbote by his creator, his lonely mind invents the fantastic landscape of Zembla, which mirrors the psychological state of its self-styled "king." Even the composition of Zembla's craggy mountain range embodies and reflects Kinbote's preoccupation with male beauty and masculine sex: "The Bera Range, an erection of veined stone and shaggy firs, rose before me in all its power and pride" (p. 259). ("Bera" is, of course, an anagram of "bare" and more than Kinbote's soul is being bared in this particular sentence.)

In the Commentary, which relays irrelevant, trivial, or totally useless information with regard to Shade's poem, Kinbote unwittingly reveals his own unique character. In a typically trivial note, for example, he cites the passage in *Pale Fire* where Shade describes his habit of shaving in the bathtub. In his note, Kinbote remarks that he has, in fact, witnessed this ritual procedure: "I was going to Washington and just before starting remembered [Shade] had said he wanted me to look up something in the Library of Congress. I hear so clearly in my mind's ear Sybil's cool voice saying: 'But John cannot see you, he is in his bath'; and John's raucous roar coming from the bathroom: 'Let him in, Sybil, he won't rape me!' But neither he nor I could recall what that something was" (p. 264). What we really learn here is how John and Sybil Shade react to the persistent attentions of their eccentric neighbor. Sybil tries to shield her husband from Kinbote's enthusiastic interest, but Shade remains kindly, amused, and unselfconscious around his homosexual neighbor. Kinbote, for his part, is often busy snooping around the Shades' domicile, stalking the poet whenever his wife has left him alone. One day, returning home, Kinbote meets "Sybil speeding townward" in her car. He goes directly to Shade's house "to see what my dear neighbor was doing"; here he resembles, by his own description, "a lean wary lover taking advantage of a young husband's being alone in the house!" (p. 287). Kinbote snickers at his own description, because he regards his friendship for Shade as sheerly platonic. He is not physically attracted to the aging and overweight poet, but reveres Shade's creative genius and wildly hopes he is applying it to the composition of a poem about Zembla. Kinbote's little jest characteristically backfires on the teller. *Pale Fire* is not about Zembla, and Kinbote's lofty intimacy with the poet is little more than a boyish daydream. Throughout the novel, Kinbote comically, and mistakenly, casts his relations with the Shades in the form of a tight little triangle—with Sybil the pear-shaped obstacle to artistic rapport, intellectual camaraderie, and male freedom.

Amusing ironies often arise in the Commentary from the ostentatious, but unconvincing, display of dignity with which Kinbote embellishes his most scurrilous activities as peeping Tom and woman-hater. Even the "something" Shade has allegedly requested from the Library of Congress appears to be Kinbote's trumped-up excuse for turning up, once again, at Shade's door. The reader's skepticism is reinforced by the discovery that neither Shade nor Kinbote can remember what "that something was." Kinbote repeatedly employs different ruses and excuses to penetrate the protective walls of the Shades' household. He even describes his various methods for besieging this stronghold of matrimonial bliss: "After not having seen [Shade] for a couple of days, I happened to be bringing him some third-class mail from his box on the road, adjacent to Goldsworth's (which I used to ignore, crammed as it was with leaflets, local advertisements, commercial catalogues, and that kind of trash) and ran into Sybil whom a shrub had screened from my falcon eye" (p. 86). The attentive reader will note that Kinbote is considerately bringing to Shade the very "third-class" junk mail that he leaves disregarded, and unopened, in the Goldsworths' overstuffed mailbox. (Lonely Kinbote, who has no qualms about leaving the Goldsworths' mailbox virtually inoperative, apparently has no reason to expect a letter addressed to him.) Quite understandably, Sybil Shade tells Kinbote "not to bother [John] with those ads." Failing, this time, to gain admission, Kinbote returns to one of his numerous perches, from where—at a window, on his veranda, or "from behind a tulip tree"—he may glimpse his poet (p. 87).

Through the distorting prism of Kinbote's private obsessions, John Shade's hale and hearty presence radiates life. Between the lines of bizarre Commentary we glimpse what Kinbote often misses: the poet's lucid perceptions. We even glean how well Shade understands his eccentric neighbor, despite the fact that Shade is intensely preoccupied with the composition of his poem *Pale Fire*. When, for instance, Kinbote finds himself on the verge of divulging his "true identity" as King Charles, which he presumes he has hidden from Shade, the poet kindly remarks, "I think I guessed your secret quite some time ago" (p. 288). At the Faculty Club, when the subject of Zembla's king comes up (according to Kinbote's arrangement of the "facts," at least), Shade teasingly comments, "Kings do not die—they only disappear, eh, Charles?" Like Ardalion in *Despair*, Shade is not interested in the subject of resemblance, a subject that obsesses Kinbote. Shade says, "Resemblances are the shadows of differences. Different people see different similarities and similar differences" (pp. 265-266).[18]

One of the most interesting effects of Shade's powerful presence within the context of Kinbote's Commentary is the way the poet's compassion for his mad neighbor informs and enlarges the reader's own perception of Kinbote. While Kinbote remains blind to the essential realities of Shade's life, marriage and the very poem he cherishes, the poet's luminous shade (Clare Obscure in a very different sense) inspires sympathy and understanding for Kinbote's own plight. Despite his admiration for Shade's genius, Kinbote is always selfish, if not basely ignoble, in his attitudes and behavior toward the poet. After he abandons Shade to his death, Kinbote even takes advantage of Sybil's "moment of grateful grief" to keep possession of her husband's manuscript (p. 298). Shade's penetrating perception of Kinbote, however, operates as a vital force of humane understanding within the novel: "That is the wrong word," Shade is reported to have said to a party guest who, we realize, has referred to Charles as crazy. "One should not apply it to a person who deliberately peels off a drab and unhappy past and replaces it with a brilliant invention. That's merely turning a new leaf with the left hand" (p. 238). The dead man's insight remains vital to our reading of *Pale Fire*, inspiring us to apprehend, behind the screen of Kinbote's pomposity and silly affectation, the unfortunate soul whom all this bravado is meant to hide.

Shade's poem is the bond that links, so tenuously, the disparate lives of its author and its commentator. It serves as a subtle but lucid background for the startling patterns of Kinbote's obsessed mind. As Kinbote's wild associations and impulses trace their course over Shade's creation, we perceive the psychic distance stretching between two discrete souls. While John Shade has fashioned his poem into a window for peering beyond the limits of the present, Charles Kinbote gazes through its prisms to discover a remote and mythical past. The tenuous relationship between Shade's poem and Kinbote's Commentary, which has disturbed many of the novel's readers, is itself a dramatic illustration of the essential singularity of human nature and perception. By straining to make out some intimate link or hidden bond between the identities of Shade and Kinbote, or of Shade and his author, we only perpetrate the law of averages, obscuring the nature of each character's unique reality.

"Resemblances are," in John Shade's words, "the shadows of differences." And the double, we might add, is only a shadow of the real individual, perceived in this ghostly guise by a consciousness obsessed with resemblance. To appreciate the intricacies of Nabokov's artifice, we should alert ourselves to differences, discriminate more than we compare, discern rather than generalize. We must consciously distinguish each character's uniquely delineated perception of the world. We must also be careful to discriminate between the subjective nature of a particular character's perception and his author's superior vantage within the "invented habitus." Here the self-conscious design of the fiction will have a liberating effect on the reader, as the patterns of artifice provide a perspective on reality that both reveals and transcends the narrow perception of a Kinbote or a Hermann. Finally, Nabokov's readers must distinguish between the acknowledged status of the fiction *qua* fiction and, on the other hand, the rich and suggestive reality of those characters whose rendered perceptions give life to their world. The emphasis is always on perception, on sight as a form of insight which transforms detail into significance, ignorance into a form of revelation. The reader is called upon to exercise his own powers of perception, and the degree of energy and knowledge he can bring to the task is at least partly responsible for the psychological and moral insights forthcoming. These insights—the very truths of our existence—are themselves a product of human perception. Neither absolute nor objective in nature, they are, nonetheless, discoverable to man.

CHAPTER VI

❧

The Question of Realism

Before turning, in the succeeding chapter, to the complexities of *Ada*, I should like to diverge briefly from textual analysis in order to discuss more fully the literary implications of Nabokov's approach to reality. So far I have focused on the epistemological, psychological, and moral implications of his commitment to individual or "true" reality. Now, taking that speculative pause announced to the reader in my prefatory remarks, I hope to demonstrate how this commitment to unique rather than "average" reality aligns Nabokov's fiction, in unexpected ways, with the origins and development of the novel as a genre. Throughout his literary career Nabokov was singularly aware of the novelistic conventions that his own fictions so radically unsettle. As I have noted in previous chapters, he was especially sensitive to the process by which each novelist's uniquely discovered "truth" gradually fades into general idea. Clichés are, after all, the husks of once vital perception. In Nabokov's view, the novelist must oppose this entropic tendency by exploding conventional postulations of reality and discovering new sources of life. His own character Sebastian Knight appears to represent such a novelist. In a frequently quoted passage from *The Real Life of Sebastian Knight*, the narrator observes: "Sebastian Knight was ever hunting out the things which had once been fresh and bright but which were now worn to a thread, dead things among living ones; dead things shamming life, painted and re-painted, continuing to be accepted by lazy minds serenely unaware of the fraud . . . For Sebastian Knight, the merest trifle, as, say, the adopted method of a detective story, became a bloated and malodorous corpse."[1] Interestingly enough, the image of a "malodorous corpse" occurs in another discussion of the novelist's enterprise—in the well-known essay by Mary McCarthy that I cited earlier. McCarthy asserts that in *The Brothers Karamazov* the "stink of Father Zossima"—that is, the stink of the alleged saint's demonstrably mortal corpse—"is the natural, generic smell of the novel."[2] To McCarthy, the "stink" of decay is a "generic smell" because the novel's world simulates the natural laws that govern our own. Here, as elsewhere, she explicitly identifies the genre of the novel with the temper and methods of realism. Nabokov's approach, on the other hand, resembles that of his character Knight, who believes that any "adopted form" of the novel may lose its freshness as a method and die the death of respectability, becoming a conventional model rather than a lively literary mode. To mix McCarthy's and Nabokov's metaphors for our own purposes—the smell one detects in certain novels might very well arise from the bloated and malodorous corpse of a literary form no longer showing vital signs of life. In such cases, a novel's natural odor may reflect a geriatric rather than generic condition. At any rate, we should not assume, as some critics have, that Nabokov's impatience with the methods of formal realism reveals a contempt for the novel per se. Contrary to Frank Kermode's suggestion, the novel as a literary form was never the object of Nabokov's disdain.[3] For Nabokov, composing a novel was a creative exercise demanding constant engagement with, and revitalization of, literary tradition. His impulse to parody and undermine the conventions of old novels was itself an expression of that literary rebelliousness which, from the time of Cervantes, has characterized many of the novel's greatest practitioners.

The first novelists in Europe and England were, as Ian Watt has pointed out, rebelling against accepted ways of viewing and depicting reality. In *The Rise of the Novel*, Watt identifies the techniques of literary realism with "the general temper of philosophical realism" that developed in the West during the Renaissance: "Modern realism, of course, begins from the position that truth can be discovered by the individual through his senses: it has its origins in Descartes and Locke . . . The general temper of philosophical realism has been critical, anti-traditional and innovating; its method has been the study of the particulars of experience by the individual investigator, who, ideally at least, is free from the body of past assumptions and traditional beliefs." Whereas "previous literary forms had reflected the general tendency of their cultures to make conformity to traditional practice the major test of truth," the novelist's primary criterion became "truth to individual experience—individual experience which is always unique and therefore new."[4] With regard to Nabokov's practice as a novelist, his emphasis on the reality of individual experience and his rejection of accepted models surely ally his fiction, in significant ways, with the development of philosophical realism. If, as Watt says, literary realism grew out of the tendency for "individual experience to replace collective tradition as the ultimate arbiter of reality," then Nabokov may be called a realist par excellence.[5] Discarding collective formulations of truth, he sought to locate reality at the point where the individual's perceptions diverge from the common view, conceiving personal meaning out of unique experience. To describe Nabokov as a realist, however, obviously places him in a paradoxical position with regard to what we call formal realism, a set of literary conventions that evolved from the practice of philosophical realism.[6]

Ford Madox Ford once complained that "the trouble with the English nuvvelist from Fielding to Meredith, is that not one of them cares whether you believe in their characters or not."[7] Like Henry James before him, Ford objected to the novelist's assumption of the storyteller's role. He must not confess to dealing in make-believe rather than reality. Convinced that the novel's special power depends on its illusory continuity with daily life, James has obviously had a lasting influence on generations of readers and critics:

It [fiction] must take itself seriously for the public to
take it so . . . The only reason for the existence of a
novel is that it does attempt to represent life . . . Certain accomplished novelists have a habit of giving
themselves away which must often bring tears to the
eyes of people who take fiction seriously . . . In a di-
gression, a parenthesis or an aside, he concedes to the
reader that he and this trusting friend are only "making believe." He admits that the events he narrates
have not really happened, and that he can give his
narrative any turn the reader may like best. Such a
betrayal of a sacred office seems to me, I confess, a
terrible crime . . . It implies that the novelist is less
occupied in looking for the truth (the truth, of course
I mean, that he assumes, the premises that we must
grant him, whatever they may be) than the historian
. . . To represent and illustrate the past, the actions of
men, is the task of either writer . . .[8]

In his parenthetical remark near the end of this passage, James concedes the inherent subjectivity of any
novelist's pursuit and rendering of truth; it is based,
after all, on his personal "premises." James nevertheless stresses that the inherent subjectivity of fiction
should be deliberately obscured by its realistic presentation, so that the autonomous process of history
—of actual rather than created events—appears to be
unfolding before us. Only if the novelist sustains this
illusion will his particular truth be taken seriously.
History is for adults, make-believe for children.

James, of course, understood the importance of the
artist's imagination and his craft, just as he knew that
fiction does not simply unfold before us the recorded
"actions of men." He believed, however, that the artist must apply his imaginative resources toward sus-

taining the illusion and appearances of historical process. Before James and the great age of the realistic
novel, Laurence Sterne had already challenged such
assumptions in *Tristram Shandy*. Not only did Sterne
dramatize the problems of recording the actions of
men (let alone their wayward internal lives), he also
allowed his characters to debate the question of historical authenticity versus the make-believe of fiction. In a telling passage from Sterne's novel, Trim
reads aloud from Yorick's sermon, which includes a
"poetical" description of the horrors of the Inquisi-
tion. Trim is moved to tears by the affecting scene
pictured by Yorick. It describes a "melancholy wretch
. . . just brought forth to undergo the anguish of a
mock trial, and endure the utmost pains that a studied system of cruelty has been able to invent." Trim is
grievously affected by Yorick's description; Walter
Shandy and Dr. Slop try to comfort Trim by assuring
him that this is, after all, a literary invention rather
than historical reality: "I tell thee, *Trim*, again, quoth
my father, 'tis not an historical account,—'tis a description.—'Tis only a description, honest man,
quoth *Slop*, there's not a word of truth in it.—That's
another story, replied my father."[9] Walter Shandy
and Dr. Slop attempt to quell Trim's anguish by employing the familiar argument that make-believe is
not inherently serious. Carried away by this line of
reasoning (and, perhaps, by his Catholicism), Dr.
Slop would dismiss any claim to truth on the part of
fiction (unwittingly condemning, of course, the very
nature of his own existence in the novel). Insofar as
the argument may succeed in comforting Trim, Walter Shandy goes along with it; but he stops short of

denying fiction its "truth." In more ways than one, the discovery of truth is itself "another story."

Despite the evidence provided by Sterne and other self-conscious writers, both past and present, James's contention that fiction should present itself as re-corded history still operates as a primary assumption for many critics of the novel. Watt, for example, con-tends that Fielding's self-conscious references in the introductory chapters of *Tom Jones* "tend to diminish the authenticity of his narrative." In Watt's opinion, Fielding "underestimated the connection between truth and the maintenance of the reader's 'historical faith.' " His "ironical attitude towards the reality of his creation"—that is, his treatment of *Tom Jones* as a "comic epic in prose" rather than as recorded history —detracts from the novel's "moral significance." Watt, therefore, finds Fielding's self-conscious mode of narration "deficient" and regrets that the author did not convey his truth "through character and ac-tion alone, and could only supply it by means of a somewhat intrusive patterning of the plot and by direct editorial commentary."[10]

Nabokov has also been censured for his self-indul-gent patterns, intrusive authorial voice, and failure to leave his characters on their own.[11] His departure from the methods of formal realism reveals his basic disagreement with the underlying assumptions of writers and critics who seek literal authenticity and the reader's "historical faith" in the novels they read. Challenging the assumptions of James, Watt, and McCarthy, to name but a few, Nabokov maintained that all versions of lived events—whether they ap-pear in historical accounts, in the current newspaper, or in novels—are fictions. There is no story, or history, without a teller; there is no "truth" for which human consciousness is not responsible. "I do not believe," he said, "that 'history' exists apart from the historian."[12] Why, he might have added, should fiction pose as something that cannot exist in reality? Nabokov's self-conscious mode of fiction is, quite obviously, a truthful reflection of *his* assessment of reality, based on his particular premises. Rejecting the notion of life-in-general, Nabokov insisted that "life does not exist without a possessive epithet."[13] He refused to abstract "life" from the particular individual whose consciousness informs it. This commitment to the singularity of human perception governed Nabokov's definition of reality and his methods for rendering such reality in his fiction.

In his treatment of sight as insight and of perception as intrinsically psychological, Nabokov actually developed, in a radical way, Henry James's celebrated method of rendering individual consciousness within the novel. The psychology of perception is, as Dorothy Van Ghent has shown, both the subject of *The Portrait of a Lady* and the basis for its narrative method:

> The title, *The Portrait*, asks the eye to see. And the handling of the book is in terms of seeing. The informing and strengthening of the eye of the mind is the theme—the ultimate knowledge, the thing finally "seen," having only the contingent importance of stimulating a more subtle and various activity of perception . . .
>
> In James' handling of the richly qualitative setting, it is characteristically significant that he suggests visual or scenic traits almost always in such a way that

the emphasis is on *modulations of perception in the observer*. The "look" of things is a response of consciousness and varies with the observer; the "look" of things has thus the double duty of representing external stimuli, by indirection in their passage through consciousness, and of representing the observer himself.[14]

Every item perceived by Nabokov's narrators and protagonists similarly acts as a mirror of the observer's consciousness. The effect of Nabokov's self-conscious method is to suggest, furthermore, that objects are subjective mirrors in *reality* as well as in art, because for Nabokov the world is not an objective entity but a "universe embraced by consciousness." By arranging the details of his literary landscape as reflections of their very observers, Nabokov made James's "modulations of perception"—or, as he called them, "the shifts of levels" of perception—the very form and context of human reality. By doing so, he was led to present his own fictions not as objective, historical worlds but as verbal mirrors and suggestive fairy tales. The result was, paradoxically, to violate the laws of formal realism and, in James's words, to betray the novelist's "sacred office."

In essential agreement with James on this matter, Ian Watt makes some incisive comments, nonetheless, on the dangers inherent in formal realism—dangers arising from the temptation to have fairy tales masquerade as objective reality. Watt points out, for example, that Samuel Richardson's eighteenth-century epistolary novel *Pamela* is really a "modern variant" of the age-old fairy tale *Cinderella*. But in *Pamela*, the narration includes so "full a background" and

such "minute-by-minute details" that the devices of
formal realism lend a false "air of authenticity" to the
"improbable" romance. Watt observes that the ap-
peal of most popular novels stems from a similar use
of realistic devices to create "an unreal flattery of the
reader's dreams." Watt concludes: "For this reason,
the popular novel is obviously liable to severe moral
censure where the fairy story or the romance is not: it
pretends to be something else, and . . . it confuses the
differences between reality and dream more insidi-
ously than any previous fiction."[15]

The notion of probability appears to be a central
criterion for distinguishing between the degrading
influences of popular novels and the laudable effects
of serious ones. In Watt's view, the illusion of literal
authenticity should not be used to lend an "air of
authenticity" to improbable dreams and unlikely
events. But as Nabokov frequently maintained, notions of probability are themselves subjective and
subject to question. The probable is often confused
with the familiar, and with accepted values and conventional wisdom that may obscure the nature of
individual reality. James, we recall, assumed that the
novelist's version of reality is based on his personal
premises. Yet he insisted that all novelists must do, in
their own way, what Richardson does in *Pamela*—
fashion a subjective vision of reality into a semblance
of literal truth and actual history. Many an author's
vision of reality is obviously more noble and complex
than Richardson's in *Pamela*. Yet once the notion of
probability is called into question, as it was by Nabokov, Watt's criticism of the popular novel may be ap-

plied to the central assumptions of formal realism as well. Nabokov, who found that even recorded history may be a kind of romance, or fiction, was understandably averse to *any* literary method that aspires to the authenticity of ultimate and objective reality. Not only may such literature pander to our most passive desires for escape; but by purporting to reproduce reality in universal form, it obscures its individual nature and origins. Moreover, formal realism's formidable "air of authenticity" may lead the individual to a passive acceptance of things as they are (that is, as they are purported to be), severing him from his own finest perceptions, which are conceived only in energetic resistance to the status quo.

Despite, or perhaps because of, his break with the conventions of formal realism, Nabokov was in a special position to renew the challenges raised by earlier novelists against exhausted cultural formulations of reality. Like James before him, he created the kind of "difficult" fiction that the French critic Roland Barthes defines as a "text of bliss" rather than a "text of pleasure." Barthes notes the distinguishing characteristics of each of these types: "Text of pleasure: the text that contents, fills, grants euphoria; the text that comes from culture and does not break with it, is linked to a *comfortable* practice of reading. Text of bliss: the text that imposes a state of loss, the text that discomforts . . . , unsettles the reader's historical, cultural, psychological assumptions, the consistency of his tastes, values, memories, brings to a crisis his relation with language."[16] The notion of "aesthetic bliss," frequently quoted in conjunction with Nabokov's fiction, is here appropriately expanded, I think, by Barthes's understanding of the break with comfortable formulations that heightened awareness brings about. Insisting on the priority of consciousness within reality itself, Nabokov challenges our current "historical, cultural, [and] psychological assumptions" about it.

Like his character Sebastian Knight, Nabokov approached the writing of novels as an act of continual discovery, as a problem to which there is no fixed solution. Literature must constantly be renewed as unique forms of perception gradually fade into fixed formulations and are subsumed by average reality. From this point of view, all "texts of bliss" are transformed by time into "texts of pleasure," as they settle into respectable adulthood. (Something like this has certainly happened to *Lolita*; the once-outlawed nymphet has traveled, in a very short time, from the pages of the *demi-mondaine* Olympia Press to the solid propriety of an impressive annotated edition.) Perhaps much of the hostile criticism directed at Nabokov's fiction is simply testimony to the fact that most of his novels are still extremely vital texts of bliss. It is in the nature of all serious novelists, I believe, to aspire to create such texts of bliss. There has never been, after all, a single kind or form of novel. What has defined these multifarious extended works of prose fiction as novels is not so much a particular form as an inherent spirit, expressed in the novelist's continuing search for an "appropriate form" in which to embody and examine reality. In pursuit of this elusive reality, the novelist has continued to unsettle our most entrenched assumptions and our faith in adopted cultural formulations. If this is the essential legacy created and developed by generations of novelists, it is a "tradition" to which Vladimir Nabokov unquestionably belongs.

CHAPTER VII

❦

Heaven, Hell, and the Realm of Art: *Ada*'s Dark Paradise

The world of *Ada* has been made strange by art, its landscape saturated with an atmosphere of make-believe that Henry James and his followers would surely deplore. The artifice is more intricately contrived, the self-conscious allusions more densely woven than in any previous, or subsequent, novel by Nabokov.[1] Every item of Antiterra's social, historical, and geographical reality has been patently arranged by the author, who has distorted and recombined the familiar elements of terrestrial existence. In no other novel did Nabokov more deliberately disengage his "invented habitus" from the sphere of quotidian existence, our daily struggle with seemingly intractable material and social conditions. At first glance, then, *Ada* would appear to have fulfilled the expectations of so many of his critics: on Antiterra, or Demonia, the only perceptible values seem to be aesthetic ones.[2] A more prolonged contemplation of *Ada*'s world, however, elicits responses which are not so easily categorized. As I hope to demonstrate, *Ada*'s carefully arranged aesthetic effects offer us fresh perceptions of our own psychic world and the way it is structured. Employing the techniques of artifice, Nabokov estranges us from our overriding preoccupations with "average reality" and illuminates aspects of conscious life that might otherwise be taken for granted, obscured by our inattention.

While life on the planet Antiterra does not resemble earthly existence in its familiar and routine guise, *Ada*'s bright surfaces and glittering creatures reflect, as they share with us, the most extreme and extraordinary states of consciousness. These comprise, in Van Veen's words, moments of "art and ardor and the ardor of art." Such ardor is, for most of earth's inhabitants, a relatively rare and special experience; the exigencies of daily life make unremitting demands on our attention, after all. Antiterrans, on the other hand, appear uniquely free of the pressing concerns that both limit and define existence on our planet. An anti-earth, Antiterra is not conceived as a speculative middle ground (occupied by our earth from the beginnings of Judeo-Christian tradition at least) between the symbolic heights of heaven and the depths of hell. The polar extremes of experience that we associate with these regions—heavenly ecstasy and hellish degradation, delight and despair—are, in the world of Antiterra, no longer kept at safe remove from each other by the familiar plane of earth's average reality. On Demonia, these two distinct symbolic spheres, scrupulously divided by aeons of space and time in the cosmogonies of earth's theologians, appear to have converged in one solitary globe—and

133

the middle range of human experience largely obliter-
ated by the intense pressure of that union.

   Because of this radical adjustment in the psychic
landscape, the inhabitants of Antiterra appear to us
as unnatural and unfamiliar as their planet's topog-
raphy. Their experience, like Antiterran history and
geography, seems a strangely distorted version of
what life, on our earth, is all about. Existing in a fer-
ment of art, the novel's central characters pursue lives
of remarkable, quite inhuman excess—an excess both
moral and material, transcending the limits of earthly
standards and expectations. The intensity, as well as
the exceptional duration, of Van and Ada Veen's
eighty-year practice of ardent incest is itself a flagrant
challenge to the reader's notion of what is possible,
let alone probable, in his own world. The Veens'
unnatural and enduring erotic obsession does not recall the mutual fidelity of earthly beings so much as
the inhuman passion, divine and cruel, of pagan gods
and goddesses. The ardor of Van and Ada is, to a
remarkable degree, unalloyed by the kinds of restraints and concessions that inhibit the course of
love among human beings on our planet.

   The Zemski family tree, of which Van and his sister
Ada are the last surviving members, actually recalls
the elaborate genealogies of mythic beings whose ancestral origins devolve, at the furthest reaches of
time, into primal divinities of elemental creation: sea,
sky, and air. Van and Ada trace their origins, in a
metaphorical sense at least, back to the primal ocean,
their "Darkblue ancestor," who takes the form of a
great-great-grandmother, Princess Sofia Temnosiniy.[3] As Van points out, the name Temnosiniy means

"dark blue" in Russian; it is, in that language, a common epithet for the sea, as "blue" (*siniy*) is for the sky (p. 9). Princess Sofia Temnosiniy's twin great-granddaughters, Aqua and Marina, have names that, not coincidentally, together form the Latin *aquamarina*, or "sea-water," a word that originally denoted the color of the Mediterranean Sea. Moreover, when comparing Marina's beauty to that of a naked nymph in a picture by Parmagianino, Demon Veen, who has been drinking with Baron d'Onsky (Demon Veen's secret rival for Marina's affections) remarks how "such nymphs were really very much alike because of their elemental limpidity" and "the similarities of young bodies of water" (p. 13). In the "Zemski group of nymphs" Van includes both Ada and her half-sister Lucette (p. 367). Describing a family reunion, Van has Demon jokingly refer to him as *filius aquae*, indirectly alluding to the fact that Aqua is supposed to be his mother (p. 243). As the great-great-grandson of Princess Temnosiniy, Van is *filius aquae*, the sea's offspring, in a special sense—despite the fact that Marina rather than Aqua is his true mother.

As the most remote branches of Van and Ada's family tree extend into the "blue" of their "Darkblue ancestor" Temnosiniy, so the Veens appear to dissolve, rather than die, into the primal elements of creation: "Three elements, fire, water, and air, destroyed, in that sequence, Marina, Lucette, and Demon. Terra waited" (p. 450). Demon Veen virtually disappears into thin air when the "gigantic flying machine" on which he is traveling "inexplicably disintegrated" in "blue air" (pp. 504-505). Lucette ventures suicide by drowning; her body, too, is never found. Having recurrently experienced her life as a mere "picture painted on air," her existence as only "a fragment, a wisp of color," Lucette suffers a death suitably incorporeal (p. 464). Figures of mysterious, elemental creation, the Veens appear to derive their special status from the very artifice in which they dwell. They are creatures fashioned by art, existing in a world of fabrication—pictures "painted on air"; and as though cognizant of the source to which they owe their very existence, most of the Veens are either connoisseurs or collectors of art. Aristocrats and virtual lords of Demonia, the Veens enjoy a life of luxury and license that is astounding by earthly standards. Moving as freely as gods through the lush landscape, they lavish their inexhaustible wealth on the pursuit, as Van puts it, of "old masters and young mistresses" (p. 4). Others, less favored or fortunate, are mainly the Veens' servants, playthings, and victims. With cool detachment, referring to himself in the third person, Van Veen observes how "no sooner did all the fond, all the frail, come into close contact with him . . . than they were bound to know anguish and calamity, unless strengthened by a strain of his father's [Demon Veen's] demon blood" (p. 20).

The myths of ancient Greece and Rome describe the devastation wrought by gods and goddesses upon mortals who come into contact with the fire of divine anger or ardor; on Van's Antiterra, or Demonia, ordinary beings suffer comparable disaster when they come into contact with the Veens' demonic passion. Van tells us that he, for one, suffers no pangs of conscience at the thought of his devastating effect upon others. To him the notion of "pity" is essentially "silly," a mere "sentiment" with which he has little acquaintance (p. 354). Without the slightest sign of hesitation or subsequent remorse, Van will break the jaw of a man who dares to caress Ada's hand at a restaurant table or brutally blind a former servant who tries to blackmail him (pp. 515-516, 445-446). As a young man, Van performs amazing feats in the guise of a mysterious acrobat, Mascodagama; these daring stunts, too, have a devastating effect upon other people: "The shock of [Mascodagama's] powerful and precipitous entry affected so deeply the children in the audience that for a long time later . . . nervous little boys and girls relived, with private accretions, something similar to the 'primordial qualm,' a shapeless nastiness, the swoosh of nameless wings, the unendurable dilation of fever which came in a cavern draft from the uncanny stage" (p. 183).

This touch of the primordial, the terrifying "swoosh of nameless wings" is a form of demonic energy apparently passed on to Van and Ada by their father Demon. Satanically hovering over the landscape with "long, black, blue-ocellated wings," Demon Veen is both majestic and mythic in his blackness (p. 180). Monstrous egotist, lascivious seducer, Demon practices a kind of carnal art; he is dedicated to "the minor poetry of the flesh" (p. 523). Impelled by "ravenous ardor," he feeds on live beauty with the same appetite that sparks his pleasure in "an especially succulent morsel" of roast fowl. Both are to be savored between his "red tongue and strong canine" (p. 256). Demon's "incestuous" pleasure at making love to Marina, his wife Aqua's twin sister, is thus rendered as an act of physical feeding and, at the same time, aesthetic play. Van describes how his father "fondled, and savored, and delicately parted and defiled, in unmentionable but fascinating ways, flesh (*une chair*) that was both that of his wife and that of his mistress . . . an orgy of epithelial alliterations" (p. 19).

Like Van and Demon, Ada Veen has a devastating effect on the frail mortals with whom she comes into close contact. Ada's beauty is as potent, evidently, as that of Venus; her many lovers are wounded by "lethal shafts" more devastating than those of Cupid (p. 320). Poor Percy de Prey, for example, is killed shortly after he abandons Ada for a distant war, while another lover, Philip Rack, dies abruptly of "voodoo" poisoning (p. 313).[4] Later, Ada marries Andrey Vinelander, and while it takes the ravages of tuberculosis a good while to kill off Andrey, his demise comes soon enough to grant Ada nearly a half-century of blissful cohabitation with Van. Within their own lifetime, Van and Ada are immortalized by the inhabitants of Ladore as local divinities of love. Many years after their "first summer in the orchards and orchidariums of Ardis," they discover that their incestuous love affair has "become a sacred and secret creed, throughout the countryside. Romantically inclined handmaids . . . adored Van, adored Ada, adored Ardis' ardors in arbors. Their swains, plucking ballads on their seven-stringed Russian lyres . . . added freshly composed lines . . . to cyclic folk songs. Eccentric police officers grew enamored with the glamour of incest." While Van (and Nabokov) enjoys making fun of the inspired nightwatchmen, worshippers of Ardis's cult, fighting "insomnia and the fire of the clap with the weapons of *Vaniada's Adventures*," there is essential truth behind the "painted word" of local legend (p. 409). For in *Ada*'s world of shimmering artifice, Van, his sister, and his princely ancestors are, like legendary figures of myth, rendered on a scale larger than life.

If, however, the prodigious gifts of Van and Ada Veen tend to raise them to the level of the superhuman, there are also times when both characters appear abysmally *in*human. These qualities are no accidental effect in the novel; they do not arise, inadvertently, from Nabokov's alleged identification with his "super-imperial" couple. Contrary to the assumptions of many of *Ada*'s critics, Nabokov rendered his main characters with extreme critical detachment; they are in no way intended to serve as his or his wife's literary doubles.[5] Understandably impressed by Van and Ada's talents, the poetry of Van's prose, and the enchantment of his love affair with Ada, critics have tended to overlook the darker elements of the Veens' experience. Their inhuman qualities are, however, deliberately set forth in the text, to be examined by the reader. Our recognition of these inhuman qualities is, I believe, as essential to an understanding of *Ada* as those subhuman elements are to *King, Queen, Knave*.

The Veens' superhuman and inhuman qualities spring from the same dynamic source. From childhood on, Van and Ada's appetites are as prodigious as their intellectual gifts. Just as there is something dark and inhuman about Van Veen's amazing stunts as Mascodagama—acrobatic feats that terrify children and make them cry—there is something "monstrous," as Van admits, about his insatiable lust and even about Ada's inordinate victories at Flavit, the Antiterran form of Scrabble (pp. 97, 223, 227). The health of these two extraordinary lovers is also phenomenal; both live past the age of ninety. At one point, Van casually mentions that Ada, "never being ill herself, could not stand the sight of an ailing stranger" (p. 526). The connection, casually implied here, between Ada's own remarkable health and her intolerance for those less fortunate is significant. Obsessed as they are by a relentless capacity for "pure passion," neither Van nor Ada has much inclination, or time, for the humbler forms of human affection. Their lifelong mutual passion is something at once greater and less than earthly love.

The Greeks distinguished between the searing fires of Eros and the warm affection that exists in families and among friends. Similarly, Van Veen distinguishes between the "inhuman" rapture of erotic passion and the "human" pleasures of affection: "How strange that when one met after a long separation a chum or fat aunt whom one had been fond of as a child the unimpaired warmth of the friendship was rediscovered at once, but with an old mistress this never happened—the human part of one's affection seemed to be swept away with the dust of inhuman passion, in a wholesale operation of demolishment" (p. 252). When Van, Ada, and their half-sister Lucette are reunited after a long separation, their excitement is not an expression of the "human" affection shared by siblings but the force of erotic desire. Van finds himself caressed by "ten eager, evil, loving long fingers belonging to two different young demons" (p. 420). Only rarely in Van and Ada's many reunions during the course of the novel is attention called to the "human part" of their affection for each other: "He held her, and kissed her, and kissed her again as if she had returned from a long and perilous journey. The sweetness of her smile was something quite unexpected and special. It was not the sly demon smile of remembered or promised ardor, but the exquisite human glow of happiness and helplessness" (p. 286). The occasion for this rare moment of human warmth is ironic, however; it takes place shortly before Van discovers that Ada has been unfaithful to him (p. 285).

On the planet Antiterra, the fury of passion sets more hearts aflame than Van and Ada Veen's. The "human" warmth that people in our world characteristically express for old friends and their fellow man scarcely exists as an emotional reality, or at least as a focus of attention, in the world of *Ada*. To the exclusion of almost everything else, the characters are obsessed with the *dementia* of ardor. The Veens are not Demonia's only "hell-rakers" and libertines; nearly every minor character in *Ada* is either inspired or victimized by infernal passion. Hardly a soul is left unscathed by the ardent practices of pederasty, nympholepsy, lesbianism, or, at the very least, simple promiscuity and adultery. Nearly everyone, from servants to stealthy heads of state, is busy fondling someone else behind a convenient tree or in a handy corner. More often than not, the object of such ardent caresses is another man's lover or spouse, a child decades younger than her (or his) adorer, or a triptych of prostitutes who have turned up for the occasion. On Antiterra, young "whorelets," beautiful and diseased, are offered to the highest bidder by their mother or older brother. Van, on his way to his final reunion with Ada, thus recalls "a depraved little girl called Lisette, in Cannes, with breasts like lovely abscesses, whose frail favors were handled by a smelly big brother in an old bathing machine" (p. 471). The repellent effect of these images is obviously deliberate here, as it is in countless other passages. Inhuman passion has little to do with the moral sphere of human affection and kindness; its blinding power is demonic, not benign.

Demon Veen's position of prominence on Antiterra is evinced by the planet's alternate name, Demonia. But Demon's influence has less to do with social authority than with his "demon blood" and the demonic energies to which it gives rise. Demon's full name is Dementiy, his nickname "Raven"; and both names allude to the satanic powers of blackness. No mere human, Demon is a "daemon lover" with an insatiable craving for the delights of the flesh (p. 180). His excesses are magnificent as well as inhuman, however; he has something of that "heroic energy" which, according to E. W. Tillyard, emanates from Milton's Satan in *Paradise Lost*.[6] This majestic monster, towering in his blackness, bears little resemblance to the stinking, often ridiculous fiends of medieval cycle plays or the disgusting devils of Hieronymus Bosch's allegorical landscapes. The king of hell, Milton's fallen archangel retains much of his heavenly splendor, especially at the beginning of the poem, when the effects of his expulsion from heaven have only begun to be felt. As Mario Praz has demonstrated in *The Romantic Agony*, the image of Satan's majestic blackness had a great influence on the Romantic concept of the hero as "majestic monster" and "sublime criminal."[7] The Romantics were intrigued by the notion of fatal beauty, of love not in its Christian or "human" sense but as a form of inhuman passion.

Alluding to this literary tradition throughout *Ada*, Nabokov borrows the name of Dementiy, or Demon, Veen from a Russian Romantic poet and novelist, Mikhail Lermontov. *Demon* is the title of a long narrative poem by Lermontov, written in 1841. It describes the ardor of a satanic archangel, Demon, who falls in love with an earthly maiden named Tamara. As Simon Karlinsky has noted, references to Lermontov's poem occur throughout *Ada*.[8] By virtue of these repeated allusions, Nabokov suggests that the Veens' "inhuman" ardor is akin to the demonic passion of Lermontov's dark prince. Nabokov, like Lermontov, is not concerned with moral allegories but with the nature of unalloyed desire, with states of pure passion that transcend or obliterate the "restraints, principles," and "consolations" of life in its everyday guise (*Ada*, p. 498). At such "inhuman" moments one does not care whether human life is preserved or destroyed. The question of intention, or of consequence, is irrelevant to that ecstasy. In the case of Lermontov's Demon, inhuman passion actually destroys the object of desire. When Demon kisses the beautiful Tamara, the "deadly poison of his kiss" overcomes her frail mortality, and she dies.[9] In much the same way, to repeat Van's description, he and Ada inadvertently destroy "all the fond, all the frail," who are not "strengthened by a strain" of their father's "demon blood."

Demon Veen's daughter Ada admits that her father

is entirely without "place or occupation in life"—
occupation, that is, in the social, intellectual, or pro-
fessional sense (p. 263). Musing over the "embarrass-
ing and disgusting details" of his father Demon's lascivious "crimes," even Van occasionally experiences
"a tinge of repulsion." Nevertheless, he adores his
libertine father, recognizing at the same time that "no
accursed generalizer," or moralizer, could possibly
understand the "vagaries" that account for such feelings. Most significant here is the connection that Van
makes between the "vagaries" of his "adoration for" a
depraved father and the elusive energies of art itself:
"No art and no genius," Van declares, "would exist
without such vagaries, and this is a final pronouncement, damning all clowns and clods" (p. 237). Permeated with such "vagaries," both the landscape of
Ada and its central characters are eminently artistic;
their pursuits occupy a place outside, or beside, the
realm of ethical, moral, and social action. The Veens
are not creatures of society but "children of Venus"
(p. 410). On Demonia, says Van, "artists are the only
gods" (p. 521); but for Van the power of art is identified with that of Eros. Each brings the disciple an experience of "supreme" reality:

> What, then, was it that raised the animal act to a
> level higher than even that of the most exact arts or
> the wildest flights of pure science? It would not be
> sufficient to say that in his lovemaking with Ada he
> discovered the pang, the *ogon'*, the agony of supreme
> "reality." Reality, better say, lost the quotes it wore
> like claws . . . The new naked reality needed no ten-
> tacle or anchor; it lasted a moment, but could be re-
> peated as often as he and she were physically able to
> make love. The color and fire of that instant reality

depended solely on Ada's identity as perceived by
him. It had nothing to do with virtue or the vanity of
virtue. (Pp. 219-220)

When engaged in "the wildest flights of pure science" and art, Van pays no more heed to "virtue or
the vanity of virtue" than he does in his ardor for
Ada. Whether conducting research on Terrology,
experimenting with literary form, or pursuing *l'absolu*
with Ada, Van is always the relentless "discoverer,
pure and passionate, and profoundly inhuman" (p.
388). To all these endeavors he applies his "athletic
strength of will, ironization of excessive emotion, and
contempt for weepy weaklings" (p. 389). In his psychiatric practice, Van is so "inhuman" a researcher
that he experiences no sympathy for his patients' suffering. He is so fascinated, for example, by the disease of chronophobia, or "time-terror," that he does
"his best not to let Mr. T. T. (the chronophobe) be
cured too hastily of his rare and important sickness"
(p. 388). What makes Van a brilliant psychiatric researcher leaves him a very poor doctor indeed. No
code of ethics apparently operates in Van's world, or
in his consciousness, to inhibit his frequently ruthless
research. On Demonia the question of human rights
and individual liberty, at least as reflected through
the prism of Van's narration, is largely irrelevant.
With the exception of the occasional remorse he feels
for Lucette's suicide (spurred on by his own rejection
of her) Van Veen shows little evidence of conscience.
He gives no thought to the unhappy objects, and victims, of his inhuman study.

Van's research is conducted, for the most part, on
members of a large population of tormented Antiter-

rans—those who simply do not "fit" in the world that confines them. Harrowed by the hell in which they perceive themselves to exist, these miserable souls long for another "more deeply moral" world to which they might escape (p. 498). They dream, in fact, of a paradise called Terra, "on the opposite side of the cosmic lane [from Demonia]," where carnal appetite and cruel pride have been expelled from grace (p. 21). Haughty Van has only scorn for those who dream of an innocent paradise from which Demonia's enchanting "demons" have been expelled. He scoffs at the notion of assigning beauty and value only to the virtuous; so parochial a concept of beauty would, he realizes, transform Antiterra's "noble iridescent creatures" into mere allegories of evil, Boschean "monsters, disgusting devils" (pp. 20-21). Van's own dream of paradise has, of course, "nothing to do with virtue or the vanity of virtue"; and it has far more to do with past delights than with future rewards.

The gardens of Ardis, where Van and Ada first discover the ecstasy of incest, exist in Van's memory as a perfect world of delight. In contrast to the Eden of Judeo-Christian myth—or to those idealized gardens of Renaissance painting where, as Van says, one finds many an "Old Master's device to keep Eden chaste" (p. 406)—the remembered bliss of Ardis has nothing to do with moral innocence. In the "arbors and ardors of Ardis," the "apple of terrible knowledge" that Van and Ada devour is no symbolic fruit but, quite literally, each other (p. 16). This act of "original joy" brings Van *to* paradise rather than expels him from it (p. 70). Ardis, the original setting for Van's discovered paradise with Ada, thus comes to represent a particular state of being rather than a specific place. Meaning, as Van says, "the point of an arrow" in Greek (p. 225), *ardis* signifies that stab of pure passion which wounds Van's flesh like Cupid's immemorial shaft, and inspires him with a new sense of reality. For Van and Ada, the word "ardis" becomes a playful synonym for their sexual organs—the "scarlet" shaft and the "tender point" which wound them with paradise (p. 334). Inhuman ecstasy brings on the only heaven Van knows, a "dark paradise" of amoral joy (p. 281).

Incest, not innocence, lies at the heart of Ada's transcendent delights. The English word "incest" derives, in fact, from the Latin *incestus*, which means not *castus*, not chaste. In Nabokov's Eden, the act of incest embodies that creative principle of inbreeding which nurtures both nature and art. Discussing a Boschean landscape, Demon Veen (characteristically indifferent to the painting's moral significance but delighted by its aesthetic charm) remarks "how passionately, how incandescently, how incestuously—*c'est le mot*—art and science meet in an insect, in a thrush, in a thistle" (p. 436). Ardis is also a "dark paradise" because, unlike the symbolic heaven of Judeo-Christian theology, its sphere is rimmed with the "lining of Hell" (p. 530). Ada's infidelity, Antiterran laws prohibiting incest (established for biological rather than moral reasons),[10] and the ravages of time all conspire to oust Van from that blissful state of paradise to a black hell of despair. Van's passion for Ada— "Adochka, *adova dochka* (Hell's daughter)"—brings him, then, a private heaven-and-hell, an oxymoronic experience of "intolerable bliss" and tender agony

147

(pp. 403, 160). Like Lermontov's Demon, Van might say to Ada, "My heaven, my hell lies in your eyes."[11]

It is not in Ada's person, however, but in "Ada's identity as perceived" by Van that paradise is to be found (p. 220). Van's physical desire for, and fulfillment in, Ada arises from his imaginative apperception of her. That is why the pursuit of ardor and of art are so closely identified in *Ada*. Nabokov, who locates the operations of consciousness at the center of reality, inverts Freud's well-known theories of sexual sublimation, according to which "the artistic aptitudes . . . are secondary sexual characters"; in *Ada* Nabokov reveals, as he does in *Lolita*, that "sex is but the ancilla of art" (*Lolita*, p. 261). Van, in middle age, almost loses Ada and paradise forever, because he initially fails to perceive in the corseted woman with "fat carmined lips" the magical nymph whose "gangling grace" first led him to heaven when he was twelve (p. 556). But memory and imagination overcome the ravages of time; by strenuously exercising his perception, Van rediscovers paradise in the "bower of his brain," discerning "Ladore's pink signature" on Ada's white thigh. "In full defiance of death," Van and Ada unite in paradise once more (pp. 391, 562). Far from resembling a theological heaven of eternal bliss, however, Van's regained paradise is still riven by the torments of a private hell:

> [Ada] never refused to help him achieve the more and more precious, because less and less frequent, gratification of a fully shared sunset. He saw reflected in her everything that his fastidious and fierce spirit sought in life. An overwhelming tenderness impelled him to kneel suddenly at her feet in dramatic, yet

utterly sincere attitudes, puzzling to anyone who might enter with a vacuum cleaner. And on the same day his other [mental] compartments and subcompartments would be teeming with longings and regrets, and plans of rape and riot. (P. 574)

In *Lolita*, Humbert Humbert tells the reader that by writing his story he hopes "to sort out the portion of hell and the portion of heaven in that strange, awful, maddening world—nymphet love" (p. 137). As Van Veen's experience so eloquently reveals, however, a highly complex and basically "incestuous" relationship exists between these extreme poles of perception: "But worst of all, while aware, and ashamed, of lusting after a sick child, [Van] felt, in an obscure twist of ancient emotions, his lust sharpened by the shame" (p. 485). During his long separations from Ada, Van's obsessive pursuit of the "ardis of ardor" often reminds the reader of desperate Humbert, blindly groping for his lost paradise by clinging, with hellish fervor, to the limbs of a frail child. There are certainly moments when the "portion" of hell in Van's experience seems to outweigh that of heaven, especially to the detached reader looking on. Take, for example, Van's description of his last visit to the Villa Venus. There, among pregnant and diseased prostitutes, Van discovers a child whose black hair and pale skin resemble the young Ada's. In the course of a ten-day visit to the decaying brothel, Van has "fondled and fouled" her repeatedly (p. 357). And in the "grease-reeking darkness" of a not even "human room," Van rediscovers, through solipsistic desire, his lost paradise amid the gruesome wrecks surrounding him:

> It was not Ardis, it was not the library, it was not
> even a human room, but merely the squalid recess
> where the bouncer had slept . . . The grand piano in
> the otherwise bare hall seemed to be playing all by
> itself but actually was being rippled by rats in quest
> of the succulent refuse placed there by the maid who
> fancied a bit of music when her cancered womb
> roused her before dawn with its familiar stab. The
> ruinous Villa no longer bore any resemblance to
> Eric's "organized dream [of universal floramors],"
> but the soft little creature in Van's desperate grasp
> was Ada. (P. 358)

Through puns, anagrams, and other forms of word-
play, Nabokov encourages the reader to contemplate
the portions of *ad*, the Russian "hell," and *dis*, the
Greek one, which comprise Van's particular heaven.
(Together *ad* and *dis* nearly form the word Ardis.)
Here in the "ruinous Villa," appalling visual images
starkly dramatize the psychological truth of these
verbal designs. While ardent Van is in his ecstasy,
Nabokov's readers are far more impressed by the
hellish atmosphere of disease and degradation. Van
can ignore it, or at least tolerate it, because he is "in
heaven" with "Ada"; but we in our more "human"
condition experience a shudder of moral repulsion.

For all the delight in art and ardor that Nabokov
creates in *Ada*, he does more than celebrate the nature of "aesthetic bliss." By deliberately and unsenti-
mentally disengaging our notions of beauty and aesthetic delight from the notion of "virtue or the vanity
of virtue," Nabokov clarifies the very source and
power of art within human life. In *Ada* he demonstrates that the "wildest flights" of art, ardor, and science spring from the same vital source: inhuman de-

sire and curiosity. He does not claim for art or the artist some idealized purpose or reality, where beauty, truth, and virtue are one and the same. After rendering a world like Antiterra, whose characters are so devoted to the "supreme" reality of art and ardor, Nabokov reverses all our expectations by illustrating just how devastating to *human* life such a world can be. Van Veen, heartlessly mocking those tormented Antiterrans who dream of a "more deeply moral" world beyond their own, describes Antiterra to Ada as "this our sufficient world." But his arrogant celebration of Demonia, "where artists are the only gods," is significantly qualified by her marginal note: "Sufficient for your purpose, Van, *entendons-nous*" (p. 21). Keeping in mind Van's purpose, and his inhuman pursuits, we may perceive how very suited to the artist's pride and passion is Antiterra, a world utterly "sufficient" for the relentless "discoverer, pure and passionate, and profoundly inhuman." Demonia is a beautiful and cruel world, in which the powerful and privileged practice every form of aesthetic and erotic indulgence at the expense of the humble, unwitting, and weak. On Demonia no solid ground, no earthly "average reality" and communal order mitigate the effects of the Veens' ravenous desire.[12] No legal restraints or moral laws serve to curb the "wildest flights" of the planet's "demonic enchanters." As Ada's wry comment suggests, Demonia may be a world "sufficient" for the purpose of inhuman art and ardor, but as a context for daily human existence it would be intolerable. On Van's planet, the Demonian appetite for supreme reality has eaten through the barriers of restraint and moderation, destroying, as well, the consolations—affection, loyalty, charity— that make relations among human beings bearable on earth.

The unsentimental view Nabokov takes of art's energies should not be read, however, as his capitulation to that dubious authority, average reality. In all of his fiction, and most particularly in *Ada*, Nabokov produces another ace from his conjuror's sleeve just as the reader begins to feel comfortable with a generalization that appears to describe, and approximate, the author's intent. Having emphasized the most devastating aspects of Antiterran existence, I must quickly acknowledge that Nabokov's planet Antiterra is blissfully free of the social and political dilemmas that vex and unnerve us here on earth. The social tranquillity of Antiterra seems directly related to the fact that its heads of state, dedicated like the Veens to the pursuit of ardor, have not wasted their demonic energies on the political sphere. Whenever Van makes a casual reference to Demonian "current affairs," the reference has explicitly sexual rather than social connotations: "It was rumored that even Gamaliel on his . . . trips to Paris, and King Victor during his still fairly regular visits to Cuba or Hecuba, and, of course, robust Lord Goal, Viceroy of France, when enjoying his randonnies all over Canady, preferred the phenomenally discreet, and in fact rather creepy, infallibility of the VPL organization [handling Very Private Letters] to such official facilities as sexually starved potentates have at their disposal for deceiving their wives" (p. 329). Perhaps because of their leaders' fascination with sexual rather than political intrigue, the inhabitants of Antiterra have enjoyed a "cloudless course of Demonian history in the twentieth century" (p. 580). No social upheavals, mass murders, or political wars have marred Demonia's political tranquillity, so conducive to the ardent pursuit of love's pleasure and art's passion. And while those miserable souls on Antiterra are tormented by the relentless practices of their planet's demonic "enchanters," their romantic idealization of "Terra the Fair" serves to jolt Nabokov's readers, inhabitants of Terra, into sudden recognition that there are worse forms of hell in this, our very own world.

On Antiterra, the only visions of life on earth are communicated through the "transcendental delirium" of Van's mad patients, whose "intercommunications" with Terra have produced comically garbled, pitifully idealized versions of the historical and social conditions with which we on earth are all too familiar:

> Ever since the eighteenth century, when a virtually bloodless revolution had dethroned the Capetians and repelled all invaders, Terra's France flourished under a couple of emperors and a series of bourgeois presidents . . . Eastward . . . a super Russia, dominating the Volga region and similar watersheds, was governed by a Sovereign Society of Solicitous Republics (or so it came through) which had superseded the Tsars, conquerors of Tartary and Trst. Last but not least, Athaulf the Future, a fair-haired giant in a natty uniform, . . . honorary captain of the French police and benevolent ally of Rus and Rome, was said to be in the act of transforming a gingerbread Germany into a great country of speedways, immaculate soldiers, brass bands and modernized barracks for misfits and their young. (P. 341)

Sheer distance, "poor acoustics," or a cosmic propagandist skilled in the unreal arts of Madison Avenue has to be responsible for this flagrantly whitewashed version of earth's history.[13] It is ruthless Van Veen, exploiting the victims of his psychiatric research, who intuits some truths about Terra that go unrecognized by his visionary patients: "Now the purpose of [Van's] novel was to suggest that Terra cheated, that all was not paradise there, that perhaps in some ways human minds and human flesh underwent on that sibling planet worse torments than on our much maligned Demonia" (p. 341). With the banal euphemism of Germany's "modernized barracks for misfits and their young" still echoing in our minds, we read this sentence with a special shock of recognition. For what Nabokov manages by distancing our world so dramatically from his created one is to make us perceive the relatively innocent, or at least somewhat modest, torments inflicted on the weak by Demonia's enchanting predators. These old-fashioned torments are mere child's play when compared to the technological engines of evil that have been devised in a century rife with "moral" idealism and "progressive" ideology. In the light of our much more "terrible knowledge," Demonia seems a rather romantic, charmingly satanic world of lust and "libelulla wings" (p. 390). It is in this sense and context, I believe, that Nabokov was prompted to call Van Veen his *"charming* villain."[14] The rapacity of Demonian appetites, like Van Veen's avowed contempt for "weepy weaklings," constitutes a moral evil that we must examine against the background of incredible destruction that has, on our own planet, been carried out in the name of social morality.

For those unable to struggle against the hell in every form of conscious existence, the communal dream of a "Next-Installment World" will continue to act as a salve for mortal torments. (Van Veen's "passionate research in terrology," p. 18, is, as the word suggests, "the study of terror" that he conducts on those Antiterrans who dream of escaping to Terra the Fair.) Yet as Van so eloquently argues in his "Texture of Time"—and here Nabokov said that he agreed with his character—the existence of the future is a false illusion.[15] Only the present and the recollected and revitalized past exist in our consciousness and have any reality in which we may believe. The paradise of Terra the Fair, envisioned by poor wretches on Antiterra, is (as Nabokov's readers know only too well) a false illusion. To earth's inhabitants Terra promises no eternal afterlife of unruffled bliss but a sphere of existence analogous to, but not identical with, that on Antiterra, where each man's life is fraught with hell and harassed by death. In *Ada*, as on earth, there is no "grief-proof sphere of existence wherefrom," as Humbert Humbert puts it, "death and truth [are] banned" (*Lolita*, p. 172). Despite Humbert's persuasive eloquence on this point, many critics persist in regarding Nabokov's artifice as a "grief-proof sphere" into which both author and reader may flee from reality. Surely *Ada*, Nabokov's most elaborate artifice, calls for a major reassessment.

Though permeated by the delights of "aesthetic

bliss," the landscape of *Ada* is no place for the escapist, the aesthete, or the weak at heart to find shelter from disturbing realities. Van Veen's paradise is no "grief-proof sphere"; death, truth, and evil are not banned by its intricate design, nor do Van's aesthetic triumphs mask his flawed humanity. Both heaven and hell exist within *Ada*'s "dark paradise," reflected in the "diamond-facets" of Nabokov's remote landscape. The patterns of artifice do not distract us from the hellish aspects of mortal existence but bring us face-to-face with their intractability. Even such godlike lovers as Van and Ada Veen must ultimately submit to the laws of organic decline. As their ardors gradually diminish in frequency, their lovemaking, like the succession of Van's secretaries, grows "plainer and plainer . . . and by the time Violet Knox broke the lackluster series Van Veen was eighty-seven and completely impotent" (p. 575). Eventually this sister and brother, for so long such grand and monstrous people, must join the ranks of "all the fond, all the frail," in their world; in the end they are mortally wounded by the most "lethal shaft" of all, the "ardis of Time" (p. 538). "You lose your immortality when you lose your memory," Van tells Ada (p. 585). Our "immortality," like the "dark paradise" Van summons through imagination and memory, is strictly man-made. Only *Ada*, Van's "immortally" recorded mortal paradise, will survive after he and Ada fade "*into* the finished book" and the reader returns to earth (p. 587). Terra awaits us all.

For Nabokov, the darker elements of conscious life may not be "packed, labeled 'Hell' and freighted away," as Marina Veen supposes (p. 253). Like Van's daring feats as Mascodagama, Nabokov's verbal acrobatics leave his audience not with comfortable assurances but with the unsettling sense of being "visitors and investigators in a strange universe, indeed, indeed" (p. 107). By manipulating the elements of artifice, Nabokov creates, and induces in us, his readers, shifting levels of perception as we contemplate his "invented habitus." And as the overlapping spheres of hell and heaven emerge through the patterns, we find ourselves confronting the paradoxes of our own condition here on this planet. The distance between Nabokov's antiworld and our own earth—between deliberate artifice and familiar experience—thus creates a psychic clearing, a speculative space through which *Ada*'s readers may renew, and inform, their perception of both.

CHAPTER VIII

❀

On the Dark Side of Aesthetic Bliss: Nabokov's Humanism

The shadows cast in *Ada*'s "dark paradise" may begin, somewhat paradoxically, to clarify Nabokov's frequently misconstrued attitudes toward art and the artist. Certainly he grants to his talented narrator, Van Veen, the status of artist; Van raptly experiences states of "aesthetic bliss" and renders them in a verbal medium with all the power and originality of literary genius. At the same time that Van gives impressive form to his imagination and memory, however, Nabokov deliberately conveys the inadequacies of his character's moral vision. Van's powers as an artist and a lover neither affirm nor imply profound wisdom and humanity. Many of Nabokov's other artists and would-be artists, those presumed "masks" of a self-advertising author, have received equally rigorous and unsentimental treatment at his hands. Among all of Nabokov's novels, there are two aesthetically obsessed characters who, between them, span a quarter-century, two continents, and the two languages of Nabokov's literary production. Focusing my discussion on these two characters, Axel Rex and Humbert Humbert, I intend to reconsider once again, and in conclusive fashion, the nature of Nabokov's alleged aestheticism.

Already in *Laughter in the Dark*, originally published (under the title *Kamera obskura*) in Russian in 1933, Nabokov unequivocally outlined the distinction between artistic talent and human virtue. Of Axel Rex (called Robert Gorn in the Russian original) the narrator observes, "And at the same time this dangerous man was, with pencil in hand, a very fine artist indeed."[1] Voicing one of Nabokov's own convictions concerning the autonomy of art, Rex affirms that "an artist must let himself be guided solely by his sense of beauty" (p. 181). Despite his Nabokovian sensitivity to beauty, however, Rex is shown by the author to be brutally insensitive to his fellow man. "The only human feeling" that Rex has ever experienced, in fact, is a particular "liking" for his young mistress. Characteristically, Rex accounts for this rare feeling in terms more suggestive of inhuman appetite than of human affection: "He took life lightly, and the only human feeling that he ever experienced was his keen liking for Margot, which he endeavored to explain to himself by her physical characteristics, by something in the odor of her skin, the epithelium of her lips, the temperature of her body" (pp. 183-184). Like Demon Veen, Rex is a connoisseur of the "poetry of the flesh." His affinity with, or foreshadowing of, the satanic Veens is also suggested by his "lusterless black hair" and powder-white skin (p. 32).

Axel Rex does not confine his inhumanly "cold,

wide-eyed curiosity" to the practices of painting and caricature, at which he admittedly excells as an artist. He also toys with his fellow creatures as if they were his puppets, fashioned by his unique powers of invention. An extreme and perverse aesthete, Rex continually seeks to turn life into art for his own amusement. Unlike his author, Nabokov, he fails to make essential distinctions between the laws of art and those of life and to define his prerogatives with respect to both. Commenting on the ghastly and premature death of "a beautiful boy full of life, with the face of an angel and the muscles of a panther," Rex says, "Viewed as a work of art, the shape of his life would not have been so perfect had he been left to grow old" (p. 182). To perceive a young boy's untimely death as formally "perfect" is certainly a monstrous application of aesthetic criteria to the conditions of life. An author may regard his character's fate in this way, but not his fellow man's. Nabokov's gradual exposure of Rex's villainy within the novel is a lucid indictment of the aesthete's confusion of values.

Delighting in the deceptions of art, Axel Rex secretly moves into a Swiss chalet with his mistress, Margot, and her rich, unwitting lover Albinus, who has recently been blinded in an automobile accident. Albinus does not suspect that he is sharing Margot with another man in the same house. Taking advantage of the blind man's affliction, Rex proceeds to transform the routines of domestic life into artful compositions. These little vignettes contain the same blend of cruelty and credulity, the same relationship between victim and victimizer, that Rex creates in his newspaper cartoon sketches. In one instance we find

Albinus seated on a chair in the sunlit drawing room. Rex, whose presence is unsuspected by the blind man, sits down opposite him; the fact that Rex is stark naked adds to his perverse delight in the deception. Rex opens the game by audibly slapping his knee, which puzzles the blind man: "Albinus, who had just raised his hand to his knitted brow, remained transfixed with uplifted arm. Then Rex bent slowly forward and touched Albinus' forehead very gently with the flowering end of the grass stem which he had just been sucking. Albinus sighed strangely and brushed away the imaginary fly. Rex tickled his lips and again Albinus made that helpless movement. This was good fun indeed" (pp. 276-277).

At this moment, Albinus's brother-in-law Paul, who has been searching for his missing relative, enters the house and discovers the cruel game: "And Paul, good-natured Paul who had never in his life hit a living creature, swung out mightily at Rex's head and got it with a tremendous bang. Rex leaped back —his face still twisted in a smile—and suddenly something very remarkable occurred: like Adam after the Fall, Rex, cowering by the white wall and grinning wanly, covered his nakedness with his hand" (p. 278). Bursting in on the outrageous scene, Paul shatters the symmetry of the cartoon composition, and with it the artist's delusion of omnipotence. The boundary between life and art is abruptly reasserted. Having toyed with Albinus as if the blind man were his own creation, Rex is suddenly exposed, physically and morally, to the sight and judgment of a fellow human being. The inhuman artist discovers himself in the ethical world. Like Adam after tasting the fruit of knowledge, Axel Rex suddenly experiences the discomfort and shame of his fallen condition. Rex's exposure—this sole instant of human shame—serves to clarify the nature of his transgression against the moral imperatives of mortal existence. As Paul leads Albinus out of captivity, Rex's illusory reign is over; deposed from his position of inhuman authority, he is now just a "naked wretch looking out of the window" (p. 279).

Although Nabokov used autocratic terms to describe his practice as an artist, calling himself the "perfect dictator in that private world" and his characters "galley slaves," he repeatedly emphasized the distinction between the spheres of art and life. Only in the realm of art did he advocate dictatorship. Outside this realm, Nabokov was committed to the freedoms of democratic life. As he said in the statement I cited at length in chapter 3, "Democracy is humanity at its best . . . because it is the natural condition of every man ever since the human mind became conscious not only of the world but of itself."[2] Like Descartes, Nabokov asserts that man thinks and therefore exists—his thought or consciousness establishing the very fact and nature of his essential being; he is, in this sense, self-created. But literary characters are not so created; they are invented by an author whose will they serve. The conditions of life in fiction are neither "natural" nor autonomous. To grant every character in a novel the right to life, liberty, and the pursuit of happiness would bring only chaos. The structure and rigors of art contradict man's rightful and "natural condition" as an autonomous agent in an ideally free state. An author gives his characters "life" and may then bring on their demise for his own purposes. No matter how resplendently alive to the imagination, an author's characters are always his instruments—the tools, and the toys, of his inhuman trade. A man who loved liberty and democracy, Nabokov was acutely aware of the artist's imaginative transgressions against the essential rights of human beings. The artist, of necessity, "sins" against his characters by ignoring that moral imperative described, two centuries ago, by Immanuel Kant. A man, said Kant, "exists as an end in himself, not merely as a means for the arbitrary use of this or that will; he must always be regarded as an end in all his actions whether aimed at himself or at other rational beings."[3] Each man's inherent freedom of self is thus defined, and limited, by the necessary recognition that no man has the right to subjugate another to carry out his will.

The apparent contradiction between the freedoms of democracy and the dictatorship of art is ethically tolerable so long as the artist recognizes, as Axel Rex does not, the limitations of his sphere of influence. By calling attention to the fictional status of the worlds he controls, Nabokov unambiguously asserts his limitations as well as his powers. Within each novel, his self-conscious devices—the intrusive authorial voice, allusions, verbal games, and reflexive patterns —call attention to the circumscribed realm of the artist's authority. It is only Nabokov's characters, not their author, who err by equating *the* world with their private formulations, losing sight of the transforming power of individual perception. Thus Dreyer, in *King, Queen, Knave*, fails to perceive

Franz and Martha's true nature because he has relegated them to predictable characters within his own scripted version of reality. In *Lolita*, Humbert Humbert is more critically deluded. Carried away by his powers of invention, Humbert—not unlike Axel Rex —attempts to subject a fellow human being to the despotic rule of aesthetic creation.

Humbert does not, admittedly, resemble Rex in temperament or intention. Rex is a cool and detached villain scarcely capable of human emotions. His mortal shame lasts but a moment, while Humbert's guilt-ridden conscience condemns him to a hell of inner torment. Yet despite Humbert's more profound humanity, he does behave toward Lolita as though she were the mere instrument of his will. Like an author dreaming up a character, Humbert despotically transforms the twelve-year-old American kid into an aesthetic mirage: "Lolita had been safely solipsized . . . I was above the tribulations of ridicule, beyond the possibilities of retribution. In my self-made seraglio, I was a radiant and robust Turk, deliberately, in the full consciousness of his freedom, postponing the moment of actually enjoying the youngest and frailest of his slaves" (*Lolita*, p. 62). Through the play of inspired imagination, Humbert invents a Lolita who, most conveniently, possesses "no will, no consciousness—indeed, no life of her own" (p. 64). In the end, Humbert's mental usurpation of Lolita's identity has very real and destructive consequences. As her sole guardian, Humbert uses all the resources at his disposal to control Lolita and hamper her freedom. When bribes and threats fail, Humbert resorts to clandestine raids on Lolita's meager savings, which she attempts to hide from him. He even burgles "eight one-dollar notes," which he finds stashed away in a book, because he fears that otherwise she "might accumulate sufficient cash to run away" (pp. 186-187).

After Lolita succeeds in escaping from Humbert, he reviews their life together; gradually he comes to recognize that during those years he "simply did not know a thing about [Lolita's] mind and that quite possibly, behind the awful juvenile clichés, there was in her a garden and a twilight, and a palace gate—dim and adorable regions which happened to be lucidly and absolutely forbidden" to him (p. 286). This remote and walled garden is the private landscape that every individual shelters within his internal life. It is that private kingdom where each of us is, like the artist, a sovereign power. Humbert ultimately recognizes that he has invaded Lolita's private kingdom and usurped her rightful claim to an independent existence. Because of this physical and psychic invasion of Lolita's privacy, Humbert understands, "something within her" has been "broken" by him (p. 234). He perceives the devastating effects that his solipsistic ardor has had on Lolita's life, and it is this understanding that lends such depth and poignancy to his narration.

Humbert's recognition of his culpability is, after all, what makes him so much more sympathetic a character to us than Axel Rex; yet at times Humbert confuses his creative gifts of perception, his artistic sensibility, with moral virtue. He even declares himself more poet than pervert when describing the tender love of "unhappy, mild, dog-eyed gentlemen" for their nymphets: "We are not sex fiends! We do not rape as good soldiers do . . . Emphatically, no killers are we. Poets never kill" (p. 90).[4] By elevating himself to the status of "pure" poet, Humbert understandably desires to remove his actions from the ethical sphere of life and consider them only as art. But these attempts prove futile; guilty Humbert must ultimately confront the violence he has wrought upon Lolita. The "simple human fact," which inhuman art cannot disguise, remains: "Dolores Haze had been deprived of her childhood by a maniac" (p. 285). Humbert's eloquent self-revelation serves to enlighten the reader as well. He may not have murdered Charlotte Haze, but in some ways Humbert has butchered Lolita's life. By the novel's end, poet or no poet, Humbert perceives his hands to be those of a mangler and a "sex fiend." Gazing at Dolly Schiller's proletarian husband, elegant and aesthetic Humbert recognizes his moral inferiority to this simple man. He writes, "His fingernails were black and broken, but the phalanges, the whole carpus, the strong shapely wrist were far, far finer than mine: I have hurt too much too many bodies with my twisted poor hands to be proud of them" (p. 276).

The power and passion of the imagination do not grant the ardent dreamer any ultimate authority over his fellow man, who has an unquestionable claim to his own dreams and desires. Paradoxically, Humbert is able to grant to Lolita, within "the refuge of art," what he denies her during their brief life together: the grace of absolute freedom. Having solipsistically denied his nymphet any "will," "consciousness," or "life of her own," Humbert is nevertheless able, in retrospect and with the detachment of the artist, to summon an image of Lolita's essential and unfettered self:

> The exquisite clarity of all her movements had its auditory counterpart in the pure ringing sound of her every stroke. The ball when it entered her aura of control became somehow whiter, its resilience somehow richer, and the instrument of precision she used upon it seemed inordinately prehensile and deliberate at the moment of clinging contact. . . My Lolita had a way of raising her bent left knee at the ample and springy start of the service cycle when there would develop and hang in the sun for a second a vital web of balance between toed foot, pristine armpit, burnished arm and far back-flung racket, as she smiled with gleaming teeth at the small globe suspended so high in the zenith of the powerful and graceful cosmos she had created for the express purpose of falling upon it with a clean resounding crack of her golden whip. (Pp. 233-234)

Humbert's use of the possessive epithet—"my Lolita" —here expresses tender affection rather than solipsistic desire. This image of Lolita, which he evokes near the end of the novel, is of a human being most perfect in her freedom. Poised in time, or eternity, commanding the space that surrounds her, Lolita reigns— "golden whip" in hand—like a figure of antique statuary.

Contemplating the exquisite clarity and grace of Lolita's movements and the "classical purity of trajectory" in her tennis serve, Humbert acknowledges both the perfection and the essential inutility of her tennis form: "Her form was, indeed, an absolutely perfect imitation of absolutely top-notch tennis—

without any utilitarian results." Any "second-rate but determined player, no matter how uncouth and incompetent," could "poke and cut his way to victory" over Lolita's elegant but inefficient strokes. Lolita's tennis, adds Humbert, "was the highest point to which I can imagine a young creature bringing the art of make-believe, although I daresay, for her it was the very geometry of basic reality" (pp. 233-234). We may fruitfully apply Humbert's descriptive terms to a consideration of Nabokov's enterprise as a novelist. For in his dedication to "the art of make-believe," to self-conscious artifice that carries no useful social messages and claims no extraliterary function, Nabokov presents us, nonetheless, with "the very geometry of basic reality." Nabokov's art celebrates human consciousness, "the only real thing in the world," and delineates its laws. These laws are not, as we have seen, identical with Nature's; they are, to repeat Charles Kinbote's phrase, "anti-Darwinian." In the realm of Nabokov's fiction, which may rival Nature but never pretends to be *her* creation, the very notion of "survival of the fittest" proves an inadequate perception of human life. Celebrating the "anti-Darwinian" laws of consciousness, Nabokov's artifice reveals, instead, that the despot is his own puppet, the murderer his own victim.

The patterns of self-conscious artifice illuminate the "geometry" of consciousness and its reality. Human consciousness is unique in the world, something fragile and at the same time infinitely powerful. And man's creations, his works of art, are shown to be as fragile and as powerful as the consciousness of which art is a supreme manifestation. Art derives its power from the elusive play of infinite consciousness in the face of death's inevitable triumph. Like Lolita's tennis form, art is, in Nabokov's words, both "futile" and "organic," not useful and mechanical.[5] Only in unique, independent, and essentially nonutilitarian forms, then, does art embody the true nature of man, who may not justifiably be subverted to serve any individual or collective will. Only by art's freedom from function will it truly "serve" us.

Through the presentation of his worlds as invented ones, his characters as "galley slaves," and himself as an author impersonating an anthropomorphic deity, Nabokov reminds us that the only power available to the artist is to create the very best, the most unique and "inhuman," art that he can. But the artist's god-like authority extends no further than the flat frame of the canvas. As he refrained from claiming great-ness, or even goodness, for some of his most talented artists, from Axel Rex to Van Veen, so Nabokov dis-dained the aesthete's suggestion that the values of art may substitute for, or eliminate, the moral impera-tives of human existence. The distortive mirror of art may only reflect life in its own way—the processes of imagination being both absolute and strictly limited. Nabokov demands from his readers the same rigor-ous detachment with which he, as an author, contem-plated the special privileges of artistic creation. We are not to be so taken with the cleverness of his charming villains, nor with the beauty of their lan-guage, that we dismiss the reality of their deeds. With regard to the prerogatives of art, Nabokov was a more rigorous moralist than many of his own inter-preters. To Humbert Humbert, his aspiring artist,

Nabokov blatantly denied any moral sympathy. Despite his character's talent, imagination, and capacity for aesthetic bliss, Nabokov called Humbert "a vain and cruel wretch who manages to appear 'touching.' That epithet, in its true, tear-iridized sense, can only apply to my poor little girl [Lolita]."[6] With her bad manners and juvenile clichés, the real Lolita offends Humbert's good taste and continental elegance. But for this Lolita Nabokov reserved his tenderness and moral sympathy. If Lolita is the victim of American pop culture, she is even more cruelly the victim of Humbert's aesthetic proclivities. Against the powerful force of his animated imagination, Lolita wields her trite toughness like a weapon. It is the shield she raises, with small success, to defend that besieged kingdom—her personal identity.

Nabokov's expressed tenderness for his "poor little girl" makes obvious what should be apparent to his readers in any case. Despite the author's subjugation of his "galley slaves" within the work of artifice, Nabokov was far from indifferent to his characters or hostile to the real human beings they so convincingly resemble. And despite the many differences between Nabokov's early Russian and later English novels, a synoptic view of these works reveals how unswerving was his commitment to certain moral as well as aesthetic principles. Keenly aware of the transgressions all human beings commit against each other as they pursue, and try to realize, their solipsistic dreams and desires, Nabokov himself was no solipsist. The very form of his fiction illustrates that the artist's private world is not coterminous with ours; he does not seek to extend his personal dominion beyond the printed page. In a recorded interview, Nabokov took the opportunity, moreover, to address the tendency of so many of his critics to label him an aesthete indifferent to humanity. He invited such critics to reassess their appraisals, confronting them with a characteristically flamboyant, albeit serious, challenge: "In fact I believe that one day a reappraiser will come and declare that, far from having been a frivolous firebird, I was a rigid moralist kicking sin, cuffing stupidity, ridiculing the vulgar and cruel—and assigning sovereign power to tenderness, talent, and pride."[7] What Nabokov does *not* say here, but explicitly demonstrates throughout his fiction, is that the artist's own talent and pride have, on more than one occasion, come under the fire of his attack. Some of Nabokov's most talented and proud artists—Axel Rex, Humbert Humbert, and Van Veen—are exposed, in their cruelty, for seeking to extend their sovereign power beyond the domain of art. Unlike their author, they do not perceive a distinction between the natural condition of human freedom and the inhuman privileges of art. Such failure of insight constitutes, for this celebrated champion of aesthetic bliss, the most lethal form of vulgarity. Misconstruing Nabokov's dedication as an artist to aesthetic bliss—failing to recognize the enduring humanistic values that inform his perception of reality—makes us liable to the same criticism.

Notes

I
The Question of Character

1. Passage cited in Andrew Field's biography, *Nabokov: His Life in Part* (New York: Viking, 1977), p. 181.

2. Nabokov's commitment to aesthetic bliss is stated in a passage, frequently quoted, from his afterword to the 1958 American edition of *Lolita*: "For me a work of fiction exists only insofar as it affords me what I shall bluntly call aesthetic bliss, that is a sense of being somehow, somewhere, connected with other states of being where art . . . is the norm." "On a Book Entitled *Lolita*," in *The Annotated Lolita*, ed. with preface, introduction, and notes by Alfred Appel, Jr. (New York: McGraw-Hill, 1970), pp. 316-317. The passage has had considerable influence on critics writing on Nabokov. The title of Frank Kermode's review of *Bend Sinister*, "Aesthetic Bliss," is an obvious indication. Kermode asserts that "the novel is too easy [for Nabokov]. It can be laboriously moulded to the shape of some moralistic obsession. Nabokov finds all this contemptible and an obstacle to aesthetic bliss." *Encounter*, 14 (1960), 81. More recently in England, Philip Toynbee, reviewing *Ada*, has reiterated more vehemently, and with far less appreciation of the author, the view that Nabokov rejects the

"function of a novelist," which "has much to do with critical appraisal . . . , with social observation; even ugh!—with morals." London *Observer*, 5 October 1969; cited in H. Grabes, *Fictitious Biographies: Vladimir Nabokov's English Novels*, trans. H. Grabes with Pamela Gliniars (The Hague: Mouton, 1977), pp. 14-15. Grabes deems Toynbee's "verdict" to be "at least partly justifiable" (p. 14).

In a more positive vein, Page Stegner, in *Escape into Aesthetics: The Art of Vladimir Nabokov* (New York: Dial, 1966), maintains that Nabokov's art expresses a "fastidious revulsion against the flesh, against the vulgarity in the world, that is escapable only in what becomes for Nabokov and his heroes a spiritual substitute—aesthetics" (p. 41). More recently and, again, far less sympathetically, Joyce Carol Oates perceives Nabokov's "fastidious revulsion" to be an expression of contempt for ordinary human beings: "Nabokov empties the universe of everything except Nabokov. He then assigns worth . . . to a few selected human beings, focusing his powerful imagination upon the happy few, lavishing contempt and energetic humor upon most other people. Nabokov exhibits the most amazing capacity for loathing that one is likely to find in serious literature." "A Personal View of Nabokov," *Saturday Review*, January 1973, p. 37. Oates's view of Nabokov as hostile to humanity was foreshadowed by Russian émigré critics half a century ago. In numerous emigre articles discussing Nabokov's Russian production during the 1930s, "the basic criticism," Simon Karlinsky reports, is "that originality and novelty of the writer's craftsmanship serve no discernible human purpose and are probably a mask covering up his indifference to his fellow humans." "Nabokov and Chekhov: The Lesser Russian Tradition," *TriQuarterly*, no. 17 (Winter 1970), p. 10. For a selection of émigré critical opinion cited in Russian, see Jane Grayson, "Appendix E: Nabokov in Russian Criticism," in *Nabokov Translated: A Comparison of Nabokov's Russian and English Prose* (Oxford: Oxford University Press, 1977), pp. 234-237.

3. William Gass, "Mirror, Mirror," *New York Review of Books*, 6 June 1968, p. 3. Along with many others, Gass finds that Nabokov's characters and words form "a world of crisp,

complex, abstract and often elegant, though finally trivial relations."

4. The suggestion for this "key" comes from Vladislav Khodasevich, whom Field cites as "Nabokov's most perceptive Russian critic": "The major émigré poet and critic Vladislav Khodasevich asserted that Nabokov really writes *only* about the creative artist, but that he does this under the guise of writing about salesmen, chess players, businessmen, and others pursuing similarly unlikely professions." *Nabokov: His Life in Art* (Boston: Little, Brown, 1967), pp. 101-102. In *Crystal Land: Artifice in Nabokov's English Novels* (Berkeley: University of California Press, 1972), Julia Bader similarly maintains that Nabokov's novels are all about art and its process. She cautions the readers not to look for "consistency of characterization" in Nabokov's creatures, who are mainly masks or "figments" of the author's creative self (pp. 58, 79, 158-159). In *Reading Nabokov* (Ithaca and London: Cornell University Press, 1974), Douglas Fowler offers the most recent version of the popular theory that Nabokov's main characters are his masks or, as Fowler variously puts it, his "alter egos," "agents," "favorites," and "equivalents" (pp. 14-15, 26, 28, 92-93, 104, 123, 129, 149, 178-179, 182, 188); Fowler also believes that "escape [from reality] is Nabokov's abiding interest," that he "desires to dismiss from *his* world everything that is esthetically inadmissible" (pp. 195, 200).

5. *Nabokov: His Life in Art*, p. 349.

6. Interview with Nabokov by anonymous reporter, 5 June 1962; rpt. in Vladimir Nabokov, *Strong Opinions* (New York: McGraw-Hill, 1973), p. 7.

7. Alfred Appel, Jr., "An Interview with Vladimir Nabokov," *Wisconsin Studies in Contemporary Literature*, 8, 2 (Spring 1967), 136.

8. Iris Murdoch presents the opposite view in "The Sublime and the Beautiful," *Yale Review*, 49 (1960), 266, 271, 256-257. She believes that the "naturalistic conception of character" is much more than a literary technique. Her approach to the novel

may serve to clarify the implicit assumptions operating in much of the negative criticism on Nabokov. Murdoch openly avows that an author who truly respects humanity and individual liberty will grant his characters apparent autonomy within the work of fiction: "A great novelist is essentially tolerant, that is, displays a real apprehension of persons other than the author as having a right to exist and to have a separate mode of being which is important and interesting to themselves." She adds: "The social scene is a life-giving framework and not a set of dead conventions . . . And the individuals portrayed in the [great] novels [of the past] are free, independent of their author, and not merely puppets in the exteriorization of some closely locked psychological conflict of his own." Martin Price has described the serious attack waged by Murdoch and other critics, including Barbara Hardy, John Bayley, and W. J. Harvey, against what Price calls "the symbolist novel." While Price's description of the symbolist novel more closely resembles a work by Virginia Woolf (he names *To the Lighthouse*) than one by Nabokov, the objections raised to both the symbolist novel and Nabokov's fiction are remarkably similar: "The symbolist novel as these critics treat it . . . has a high degree of internal coherence. So intense is the coherence that characters are denied real freedom . . . They lack the substantial, opaque solidity of real persons." By ignoring "the inevitable artifice" implied by any mode of character depiction, these critics tend to regard the disappearance of traditional modes of character portrayal as a loss of humanistic values. Their attack on the symbolist novel has, in Price's words, "often taken a confusing turn. As against schematization [in the symbolist novel], as against the coherence of the work we are offered love for persons other than ourselves, as against artfulness we are offered empiricism, liberalism, and a warm response to the energies and contingencies of the actual. The symbolist work is taken to dramatize revulsion from the messy and uncontrollable." "The Other Self: Thoughts about Character in the Novel," in *Imagined Worlds: Essays on Some English Novels and Novelists in Honour of John Butt*, ed. Maynard Mack and Ian Gregor (London: Methuen, 1968), pp. 292-293.

9. *Bend Sinister* (New York: Henry Holt, 1947), p. 122.

10. *Speak Memory: An Autobiography Revisited*, rev. ed. (New York: Putnam, 1966), p. 291; italics added.

11. "Mockings of the Master Illusionist," *Saturday Review*, 8 March 1975, p. 22.

12. "Reply to My Critics," *Encounter*, February 1966; rpt. in *Strong Opinions*, p. 264.

13. "An Interview with Vladimir Nabokov," p. 135.

14. Ibid., p. 136.

15. *Nabokov: His Life in Art*, p. 328.

16. Interview by Herbert Gold, *The Paris Review*, October 1967; rpt. in *Strong Opinions*, p. 95.

17. Letter to John Leonard, ed., *New York Times Book Review*, 7 November 1971; rpt. in *Strong Opinions*, p. 219.

18. "An Interview with Vladimir Nabokov," p. 133. As Martin Price has pointed out, "there are many authors who count on characters' taking over the direction of the work, as it were, once they come into fictional life. We need not credit every wilful surrender of the author as a real one. He may be sensitive to a deeper level of motive than he can summon at the start and wait for its emergence; the internal logic of his characters may force him to see what he did not allow himself to see that he intended." "The Other Self," p. 287.

19. "Reply to My Critics," p. 263.

II
Consciousness, Real Life, and Fairytale Freedom: *King, Queen, Knave*

1. *King, Queen, Knave*, trans. Dmitri Nabokov and rev. Vladimir Nabokov (New York: McGraw-Hill, 1968), pp. vii-viii. All subsequent references to this edition will appear in the text.

2. "The Fact in Fiction," *Partisan Review*, Summer 1960; rpt. in *The Humanist in the Bathtub* (New York: New American Li-

brary, 1964), pp. 183, 186.

3. Interview by Martin Esslin, *New York Times Book Review*, 12 May 1968; rpt. in *Strong Opinions*, p. 112.

4. *Nabokov: His Life in Art*, pp. 153, 155. Grayson similarly defines them as "cardboard characters who, like puppets, go through the motions devised for them by their creator." *Nabokov Translated*, pp. 90-91. Commenting on this alleged goal of Nabokov's "to create a world of cardboard figures, a world where *things* predominate," Carl Proffer brings other evidence to bear: "We are even told *King, Queen, Knave* is a kind of *nouveau roman*. But the sophisticated psychological characterization Nabokov uses, especially in the English version, makes this fashionable claim look ridiculous. Indeed, the heavy reliance on *specified* motivation, 'narrated monologue' (*erlebte Rede*), and interior monologue is not characteristic of the *nouveau roman*." "A New Deck for Nabokov's Knaves," *TriQuarterly*, no. 17 (Winter 1970), p. 304.

5. In his foreword to the English version of *King, Queen, Knave*, p. x, Nabokov says he suspects "that those two worthies, Balzac and Dreiser, will accuse me of gross parody," but he swears he had not read their works at the time.

6. Interview by James Mossman, *Review*, BBC-2, 4 October 1969; rpt. in *Strong Opinions*, p. 142.

7. *Speak, Memory*, p. 218. Nabokov adds, "The arms of consciousness reach out and grope, and the longer they are the better."

8. *Bend Sinister*, p. 186. This perception of reality occurs to Adam Krug, Nabokov's protagonist; but Krug's thought here echoes statements made by Nabokov himself, as n. 7 indicates.

9. Interview by Nicholas Garnham, *The Listener*, 10 October 1968; rpt. in *Strong Opinions*, p. 118.

10. *Sborniki po teorii poeticheskogo iazyka* (Petrograd, 1919), pp. 101-114; rpt. in Russian, with German trans., in *Texte der russischen Formalisten*, ed. Witold Kośny, 2 vols. (Munich: Wilhelm Fink, 1969), 1, pp. 10-12, 14. Passage from Tolstoy's diary

occurs in entry dated 1 March 1897, in *Polnoe sobranie sochine-nii*, 90 vols. (Moscow: Gosizdat, 1928-53), 53, p. 141. My translations.

11. The "musical phantasmagoria" is an example of the kind of banal art that Nabokov definitively damns in his explication of the Russian word *poshlost'*, pronounced "poshlust." In *Nikolai Gogol* (New York: New Directions, 1944), Nabokov says that *poshlost'* "is not only the obviously trashy but also the falsely important, the falsely beautiful, the falsely clever, the falsely attractive" (p. 70). The essence of *poshlost'* is succinctly rendered in a sentence describing the resort town that Dreyer, Martha, and Franz visit near the end of the novel: "As the distance from the beach increased, the names [of the hotels] grew more and more poetical" (p. 232).

12. Monkeys turn up in various guises in this novel. Dreyer playfully gives Martha a monkey for a pet when courting her, but she is not amused: "Before leaving for Berlin he gave her a monkey which she loathed; fortunately a handsome young cousin with whom she had gone rather far . . . taught it to light matches, its little jersey caught fire, and the clumsy animal had to be destroyed" (p. 66). Here, too, Nabokov emphasizes the inhuman cruelty that attends the confusion of animal and human spheres of existence. In this case, the blurring of distinctions between man and animal incurs destruction as well as degradation. Maliciously encouraged to play at being a man, the monkey perishes. Playing at or with human life is always a dangerous business.

13. *Speak, Memory*, p. 33.

14. "On Learning Russian," *The Wellesley Magazine*, April 1945; cited in *Nabokov: His Life in Art*, p. 376.

15. Interview by Martha Duffy and R. Z. Sheppard, *Time*, 23 May 1969; rpt. in more complete form in *Strong Opinions*, p. 124.

16. "The Fact in Fiction," p. 182.

17. The paradoxical relationship between social and ontological power is suggested by Nabokov when he discusses Lenin and

Joyce: "Lenin's life differs from, say, James Joyce's as much as a handful of gravel does from a blue diamond, although both men were exiles in Switzerland and both wrote a vast number of words." Interview by Nicholas Garnham, p. 119. The elements common to both lives are found in the bedrock of social and historical conditions from which Joyce and Lenin emerged. To Nabokov, Joyce has fused the properties of those elements, like carbon, into a lucid diamond. It no longers resembles—even materially—the scattered gravel of Lenin's world. In Nabokov's view, Lenin, for all his professed dedication to the abstract good of the masses, lacked this capacity to fuse manifold existence into radiantly conscious life.

18. In *Nabokov's Dark Cinema* (New York: Oxford University Press, 1974), Alfred Appel, Jr., discovers the similar use of light and shadow in the *film noir* of the forties. He describes how strips of light filtered through venetian blinds, creating barred shadows, suggest an atmosphere of confinement and doom (pp. 223-228). In Nabokov's novel, however, this pattern of confinement is not a general element of the setting so much as the specific reflection of Martha's consciousness.

19. *Pale Fire* (New York: Putnam, 1962), p. 234.

20. In "A New Deck for Nabokov's Knaves," Carl Proffer singles out this portion of Franz's interior monologue as especially puzzling: "We are told that Dreyer divides into two in Franz's mind, the second Dreyer a purely schematic double—no more than 'a stylized playing card, a heraldic design' (p. 177). What does this mean?" (p. 304). I hope I have managed to suggest what the schematization of Dreyer means here.

21. Interview by Alvin Toffler, *Playboy*, January 1964; rpt. in *Strong Opinions*, p. 42.

22. "On Sirin" (1937), trans. Michael H. Walker; rpt. in abridged form in *TriQuarterly*, no. 17 (Winter 1970), pp. 99-100; also see chapter 1, n. 4.

23. Martha's perfunctory death at the end of the novel is in stark contrast to her protracted, and unsuccessful, efforts to kill

her husband. Her consciousness obsessed with death, Martha is spiritually moribund. The ease with which the "dead soul" departs from life is comically delineated in the very novel Dreyer is reading. In the case of Gogol's Public Prosecutor, only the final sundering of soul from body—that is, death—suggests that he had some kind of soul to begin with: "All these bits of talk, all these opinions and rumours . . . affected [the Public Prosecutor] to such an extent that, upon getting home, he took to brooding and brooding and suddenly, without rhyme or reason, he up and died . . . Those around him cried out . . . and sent for a doctor to let his blood, yet perceived that the Public Prosecutor was already a body bereft of its soul. Only then did they find out, with regret, that the Public Prosecutor had a soul, although out of modesty he had never flaunted it." *Dead Souls*, trans. B. G. Guerney (New York: Holt-Rinehart, 1968), p. 257.

24. *Pale Fire*, pp. 152-153, 278.

25. Interview by Martin Esslin, p. 114.

26. Alfred Appel, Jr., "Conversations with Nabokov," *Novel*, 4, 3 (Spring 1971), 216; and Appel, "An Interview with Vladimir Nabokov," p. 142.

III
Breaking the Law of Averages:
Invitation to a Beheading

1. "Anniversary Notes," Supplement to *TriQuarterly*, no. 17 (Winter 1970), p. 4.

2. Interview by Nicholas Garnham, p. 118.

3. Interview by Herbert Gold, p. 96.

4. "What Faith Means to a Resisting People," *The Wellesley Magazine*, April 1942; cited in *Nabokov: His Life in Art*, p. 375.

5. *Speak, Memory*, p. 297.

6. *Voina i mir* (Moscow: Gosizdat, 1963), bk. IV, chap. 15,

pp. 122-123. My translation. Passage cited in "Art as Device," *Texte der russischen Formalisten*, p. 22.

7. "An Interview with Vladimir Nabokov," p. 130.

8. *Invitation to a Beheading*, trans. Dmitri and Vladimir Nabokov (New York: Putnam, 1959), p. 222. All subsequent references to this edition will appear in the text. For an illuminating and comprehensive comparison of the stylistic features of the original with those of the English translation, see Robert P. Hughes, "Notes on the Translation of *Invitation to a Beheading*," *TriQuarterly*, no. 17 (Winter 1970), pp. 284-292.

9. Interviews by Herbert Gold and Martin Esslin, respectively, pp. 101, 118.

10. "The Fact in Fiction," pp. 175-176.

11. *Aspects of the Novel* (New York: Harcourt, Brace, 1927), p. 29.

12. Interview by Martin Esslin, p. 118.

13. *The Gulag Archipelago 1918-1956: An Experiment in Literary Investigation*, I-II, trans. Thomas P. Whitney (New York: Harper & Row, 1973), 419.

14. In his essay "Anya in Wonderland: Nabokov's Russified Lewis Carroll," *TriQuarterly*, no. 17 (Winter 1970), Simon Karlinsky remarks: "There was something of a hiatus in publication of Lewis Carroll in the Soviet Union in the 1920's and -30's (connected, possibly, with the anti-fantasy trend in Soviet elementary education at that time)" (p. 314). We recall that at the end of *her* trial, Alice defiantly shouts at the absurd judges: "You're nothing but a pack of cards!" Did the official Soviet censors find Alice's defiance a dangerous display of subversion? Both Nabokov's and Solzhenitsyn's treatments of the totalitarian state's mock trials call attention to the nightmarish logic made famous by Carroll's Victorian fantasy, in which the Queen of Hearts appropriately calls for the "Sentence first—verdict afterwards." *Alice's Adventures in Wonderland*, chap. 11. Nabokov published his Russian translation of *Alice* in 1923.

IV

Putting Two and One Together:
Bend Sinister

1. Introduction to *Bend Sinister* (New York: Time-Life, 1964), pp. xii-xiii. All subsequent references to this introduction will appear in the text, indicated by Roman numerals. All quotations from the novel are taken from the edition cited in chapter 1, n. 9; page references will appear in the text.

2. Nathan Rothman, "Puppet under Tyrant," *Saturday Review*, 2 August 1947, p. 33.

3. In *Nikolai Gogol*, Nabokov suggests why Gogol's Chichikov, in *Dead Souls*, and his own Monsieur Pierre use so much scent: "Chichikov himself is merely the ill-paid representative of the Devil, a traveling salesman from Hades, . . . [a] healthy-looking but inwardly shivering and rotting agent . . . The chink in Chichikov's armor, that rusty chink emitting a faint but dreadful smell . . . is the organic aperture in the devil's armor" (pp. 73-74).

4. Review of *Bend Sinister*, *The Nation*, 164 (14 June 1947), 722.

5. "Nabokov's Puppet Show, Pt. II," *New Republic*, 156, 3 (21 January 1967), 26.

6. Kenner, "Mockings of the Master Illusionist," p. 22.

7. At the close of *Bend Sinister*, a "big moth . . . with furry feet" appears at the author's window just after he has dismissed the fictional world (p. 241). In his introduction to the novel, Nabokov identifies this moth, which "bombinates in the damp dark at the bright window of [Nabokov's] room," as an image of Olga's "rosy soul" (p. xviii).

8. Trans. Max Hayward (New York: Atheneum, 1970), pp. 35-36.

9. "Aesthetic Bliss," p. 83. The title *Bend Sinister* refers to "a heraldic bar or band drawn from the left side," suggesting to Nabokov "an outline broken by refraction, a distortion in the

mirror of being, . . . a sinistral and sinister world." Introduction to *Bend Sinister*, p. xii. Kermode locates the term "bend sinister" in *Tristram Shandy*, IV, chap. 25.

10. "The Handle: *Invitation to a Beheading* and *Bend Sinister*," *TriQuarterly*, no. 17 (Winter 1970), p. 65.

11. *"Invitation to a Beheading*: Nabokov and the Art of Politics," *TriQuarterly*, no. 17 (Winter 1970), p. 46.

12. *Partisan Review*, 26, 3 (Summer 1959); rpt. in *Approaches to the Novel*, ed. Robert Scholes (San Francisco: Chandler, 1961), pp. 286, 283.

13. Ibid., p. 284.

14. Ibid., p. 287.

15. "Fortunata," in *Mimesis*, trans. Willard R. Trask (Princeton: Princeton University Press, 1953), p. 29.

V
Singularity and the Double's Pale Ghost:
From *Despair* to *Pale Fire*

1. Field states, "Nabokov is not only the foremost living practitioner of the *doppelgänger* theme, but also its most subtle and imaginative manipulator in the history of literature." *Nabokov: His Life in Art*, p. 219.

2. "An Interview with Vladimir Nabokov," p. 145.

3. Trans. Vladimir Nabokov (New York: Putnam, 1965), p. 23; italics added. All subsequent references to this edition will appear in the text.

4. Accepting Hermann's logic, Khodasevich said: "Here are shown the sufferings of a genuine, self-critical artist. He perishes because of a single mistake, because of a single slip allowed in a work which devoured all of his creative ability. In the process of creation he allowed for the possibility that the public, humanity, might not be able to understand and value his creation—and he

was ready to suffer proudly from lack of recognition. His despair is brought about by the fact that he himself turns out to be guilty of his downfall, because he is only a man of talent and not of genius." "On Sirin," pp. 99-100.

Among recent critics, Claire Rosenfield also accepts Hermann's initial assumption that he, a "breaker of the law," resembles "a poet or a stage performer." Rosenfield builds an elaborate symbolic interpretation of the novel from statements like these. She points out, for example, that "art is as early as that same first page [of the novel] equated with the illicit." *"Despair and the Lust for Immortality," Wisconsin Studies in Contemporary Literature*, 8, 2 (Spring 1967), 178. Field also takes Hermann's "analogy" seriously, observing that "the murder becomes the artist's assault upon his creation." Field concludes that Hermann's "inability to fashion himself out of his chosen image . . . is an allegory of the absurd pretension of realistic, 'representational' art." *Nabokov: His Life in Art*, p. 230. In "Nabokov: Spiral and Glass," *Novel*, 1, 2 (Winter 1968), 180, Daniel Hughes similarly concludes that the failure of Hermann's "perfect crime" is "the failure of imagination to be resourceful enough."

5. In the Russian original, it is Pushkin's short story *The Shot*, rather than Shakespeare's tragedy, that Hermann perversely inverts. In his version, Hermann says, "Sil'vio napoval bez lishnix slov ubival liubitelia chereshen i s nim—fabulu, kotoruiu ia vprochem znal otlichno." *Otchaianie* (Berlin: Petropolis, 1936), p. 45. Hermann is aware that by having Silvio kill Count B. straight off in the duel he has killed more than a character in the story; he has also destroyed the plot that unifies the several anecdotes and, of course, the moral and psychological revelation of Silvio's character.

6. Despite the numerous textual alterations made by Nabokov in the English translation of the Russian *Otchaianie*, the opening paragraph remains, significantly, very close to the original, circuitously worded Russian: "Esli by ia ne byl sovershenno uveren v svoei pisatel'skoi sile, v chudnoi svoei sposobnosti vyrazhat' s predel'nym iziashchestvom i zhivost'iu— —Tak, primerno, ia polagal nachat' svoiu povest'. Dalee ia obratil by vnimanie chitatelia na to, chto, ne bud' vo mne etoj sily, sposob-

nosti i prochego, ia by ne tol'ko otkazalsia ot opisyvaniia nedav-
nix sobytii, no i voobshche nechego bylo by opisyvat', ibo, doro-
goi chitatel', ne sluchilos' by nichego. Eto glupo, no zato iasno.
Lish' daru pronikat' v izmyshleniia zhizni, vrozhdennoi sklon-
nosti k nepreryvnomu tvorchestvu ia obiazan tem— —Tut ia
sravnil by narushitelia togo zakona, kotoryi zapreshchaet proli-
vat' krasnen'koe, s poetom, s artistom." *Otchaianie,* p. 5. Hermann's struggles with narration are presented in much the same
way in both the Russian and the English versions. For a thorough
analysis of the textual revisions made by Nabokov in the English
translation, see Carl Proffer, "From *Otchaianie* to *Despair,*"
Slavic Review, 27, 2 (June 1968), 258-267; also see *Nabokov
Translated,* pp. 59-82.

7. In *Invitation to a Beheading,* the prison officials are named
Rodion, Roman, and Rodrig. Their murderous intentions toward
Cincinnatus may well be hinted at by their suggestive names, two
of which are contained in Raskolnikov's name and patronymic—
Rodion Romanych.

8. *Prestuplenie i nakazanie* (Moscow: Khudozh. Literatura,
1970), pt. VI, chap. 2, p. 472. My translation.

9. Ibid., pt. IV, chap. 1, p. 310.

10. In *Invitation to a Beheading,* Cincinnatus's enduring self is,
quite literally, his "savior." Throughout the novel his "double"
appears at moments when Cincinnatus experiences intense fear,
grief, or disappointment. The double is that weaker aspect of
Cincinnatus's own consciousness, the victim of the present horrible moment, wanting to curl up in a ball and cry, or to step on
the face of his jailer (pp. 29, 69). When Cincinnatus's head is on
the executioner's block, the double motif recurs for the last time:
"One Cincinnatus was counting, but the other Cincinnatus had
already stopped heeding the sound of the unnecessary count
which was fading away in the distance" (p. 222). The shattering
force of fear assails Cincinnatus's psyche, refracting a false
double who, in going along with the vicious plot, nearly kills
him. Within the artifice of the novel, however, consciousness
transcends the tyranny of appearances, and Cincinnatus's real
self saves him.

11. *The Annotated Lolita*, ed. with preface, introduction, and notes by Alfred Appel, Jr. (New York: McGraw-Hill, 1970), p. 301. All subsequent references to this edition of the novel will appear in the text.

12. "The Morality of *Lolita*," *Kenyon Review*, 28, 3 (June 1966), 357, 371.

13. Alfred Appel, Jr., offers a further argument against the "symbolic" significance of Quilty's murder: "In terms of the nineteenth-century Double tale, it should not even be necessary to kill Quilty and what he represents, for Humbert has already declared his love for Lolita *before* he goes to Quilty's Pavor Manor, and, in asking the no longer nymphic Lolita to go away with him, he has transcended his obsession . . . As a 'symbolic' act, the killing is gratuitous." Introduction to *The Annotated Lolita*, p. lxv.

14. Ibid., p. lxiii.

15. In search of a "primary author" other than Nabokov, Field asserts that it "must be John Shade," whose "first voice" is that of the "craggy poet" and whose "second voice" is Kinbote's. *Nabokov: His Life in Art*, p. 300. Julia Bader similarly suggests that John Shade "has perpetrated his own 'stylistic' death within the novel, and he has then given us a new aspect of himself in the guise of another soul." *Crystal Land*, p. 31. Page Stegner, on the other hand, argues that if Kinbote is able to dream up an exotic kingdom full of "fantastic, though imaginary, personalities, he is certainly able to dream up John and Sybil Shade and their daughter Hazel, and create a fictitious poem as well." *Escape into Aesthetics*, pp. 129-130. As Robert Alter points out in his excellent chapter on *Pale Fire*, "This novel is not a Jamesian experiment in reliability of narrative point-of-view, and there is no reason to doubt the existence of the basic fictional data—the Poem and its author, on the one hand, and the mad Commentary and *its* perpetrator on the other, inverted left hand." "Nabokov's Game of Worlds," in *Partial Magic: The Novel as a Self-Conscious Genre* (Berkeley: University of California Press, 1975), p. 186.

16. Douglas Fowler, a proponent of this view (see chapter 1, n. 4), finds *Pale Fire* to be one of Nabokov's "least satisfying" fic-

tions because Kinbote does not resemble his author closely enough. Because of Kinbote's "lush homosexuality" and "egocentricity," Nabokov, in Fowler's view, "cannot give to this monster's voice the range of interest, ecstasy, wit and comedy that he himself exhibits in *Speak, Memory.*" *Reading Nabokov*, pp. 116-118. Fowler regards both John Shade and Charles Kinbote as Nabokov's doubles; but while Kinbote is an insufficient double, Shade is too good—a "spiritually flawless Nabokovian equivalent." Thus, Fowler concludes, the novel comes to a "dramatic impasse" (pp. 92-93).

17. *Pale Fire* (New York: Putnam, 1962), p. 96. All subsequent references to this edition will appear in the text.

18. Commenting on the paradoxical relationship between resemblance and difference in *Pale Fire*, Mary McCarthy observes, "Zembla, the land of seeming . . . is the antipodes of Appalachia, in real homespun democratic America, but it is also the *semblable*, the twin, as seen in a distorting glass. Semblance becomes resemblance." "Vladimir Nabokov's *Pale Fire*," *Encounter*, 19 (October 1962); rpt. as "A Bolt from the Blue," in *The Writing on the Wall and Other Literary Essays* (Harmondsworth, Middlesex: Penguin, 1973), p. 24. Keeping Shade's comment in mind, we recognize that "semblance becomes resemblance" *because* Kinbote's obsessions and fears cast their "shadows" even in the dreamworld where he has made himself king. Projecting a fantasy so seemingly "different" from his unhappy life, Kinbote nonetheless discovers, in the Zembla of his imagination, shadows (and Shadows) of the misery he has sought to escape.

VI
The Question of Realism

1. *The Real Life of Sebastian Knight* (Norfolk, Conn.: New Directions, 1941), p. 91.

2. "The Fact in Fiction," p. 176.

3. For Kermode's comments, and others', see chapter 1, n. 2.

4. *The Rise of the Novel* (Berkeley: University of California Press, 1965), pp. 12-13.

5. Ibid., p. 14.

6. As the title of F. R. Leavis's influential study of the novel, *The Great Tradition* (New York: Doubleday, 1954), implies, the experimental practices of novelists eventually produced literary works that were identified by their readers as formal models belonging to a new "collective tradition." Leavis even uses the term "classical" to describe the "tradition to which what is great in English fiction belongs." "Fielding," he says, "deserves the place of importance given him in the literary histories, but he hasn't the kind of *classical* distinction we are also invited to credit him with" (pp. 17, 11-12; italics added).

7. *The English Novel from the Earliest Days to the Death of Conrad* (London, 1930), p. 89; rpt. in *The Rise of the Novel*, p. 286.

8. "The Art of Fiction," in *The Art of Fiction and Other Essays*, ed. Morris Roberts (New York: Oxford University Press, 1948), pp. 4-6.

9. (New York: Odyssey Press, 1940), II, chap. 7, pp. 138-139.

10. *The Rise of the Novel*, pp. 285-287.

11. Fielding's dismissal by generations of critics resembles, in various ways, the consensus that has developed with regard to Nabokov's fiction. For a comprehensive discussion of critical opinion on Fielding, see Robert Alter, *Fielding and the Nature of the Novel* (Cambridge: Harvard University Press, 1968), chap. 1.

12. Interview by Philip Oakes, London *Sunday Times*, 22 June 1969; rpt. in *Strong Opinions*, p. 138.

13. Interview by Nicholas Garnham, p. 118.

14. "On *The Portrait of a Lady*," in *The English Novel: Form and Function* (New York: Harper and Row, 1953), pp. 261-262.

15. *The Rise of the Novel*, pp. 204-205.

16. *The Pleasure of the Text*, trans. Richard Miller (New York: Hill and Wang, 1975), p. 14.

VII
Heaven, Hell, and the Realm of Art:
Ada's Dark Paradise

1. See Alfred Appel, Jr., *"Ada* Described," *TriQuarterly*, no. 17 (Winter 1970), pp. 160-186; Appel provides a partial list of literary allusions on pp. 182-183 and a list of painters and paintings alluded to on p. 185, n. 2. Also see Carl Proffer, *"Ada* as Wonderland: A Glossary of Allusions to Russian Literature," *Russian Literature Triquarterly*, 3 (Spring 1972), 399-403; and Robert Alter, "Nabokov's Ardor," *Commentary*, August 1969, pp. 47-50.

2. See, for example, Hugh Kenner, "Mockings of the Master Illusionist," p. 24: "Contemplators of *Ada*'s lush verbal jungle . . . might adduce with advantage the creator of Des Esseintes [the aesthete-hero of Joris-Karl Huysmans's *A Rebours*], whose tortoises were bejeweled, and who tired of flowers and indulged in artificial flowers, and then tired of those and sought out real flowers so exotic they could pass for artificial."

3. *Ada* (New York: McGraw-Hill, 1969), p. 29. All subsequent references to this edition will appear in the text. Not coincidentally, the epithet "Darkblue" suggestively approximates the name "Darkbloom." Readers of *Lolita* will recall that "Vivian Darkbloom" is Clare Quilty's cousin, as well as an anagram of Vladimir Nabokov. By alluding to the author who has called them into being, Vivian Darkbloom and Van's "Darkblue ancestor" undermine the realistic illusion of the narrative. For a list of their "alphabetical cousins," see Alfred Appel, Jr., *The Annotated Lolita*, p. 325.

4. The strange "voodoo" poison that conveniently removes Van's rival, Philip Rack, from the scene is identified, by gruesome Doctor Fitzbishop, as "the not always lethal *'arethusoides'* " (p. 317). Arethusa is, in classical mythology, one of the Nereids—

nymphs of the Mediterranean Sea. The name of this "voodoo" poison suggestively links its magic potency to the Veens' "Darkblue ancestor" and the "Zemski group of nymphs" descended from her. The ultimate source of that potency is, of course, the author Vladimir Nabokov, the "Darkblue" (Darkbloom) ancestor from whom they all spring.

5. Perhaps because Van and Ada so little resemble the star-crossed lovers of literary tradition, trapped in a web of contingency and moral conflict, critics have been eager to see in these extraordinary creatures the simulacra of Nabokov and his wife, Vera. They assume that the Veens' extraordinary love affair, culminating in five decades of blissful cohabitation, was a celebration by the author of his own fifty years of happy marriage. See, for example, Matthew Hodgart, "Happy Families," *New York Review of Books*, 12, 10 (22 May 1969), 3. Hodgart's assumption that Van and Ada's love affair is modeled after Nabokov's own marriage met with the author's indignant protest; he pointed out that the Veens are "both rather horrible creatures." Letter to the editor, *New York Review of Books*, 13, 1 (10 July 1969), 36. Nabokov's detachment from his own characters suggests how mistaken are critics who regard his characters as the author's "masks." In *Reading Nabokov*, Douglas Fowler asserts, nevertheless, that Van Veen is "not an objectively realized character, he is a mask" for "Vladimir Vladimirovich, Nabokov himself" (p. 182).

6. *Milton* (London: Chatto and Windus, 1930), p. 277; rpt. in Praz, *The Romantic Agony*, trans. Angus Davidson (1933; rpt. 2nd ed. New York: World, 1956), pp. 55-56.

7. Praz discusses Baudelaire's admiration for Milton's Satan, "le plus parfait type de Beauté virile," on p. 30.

8. In his review of *Ada*, "Nabokov's Russian Games," *New York Times Book Review*, 18 April 1971, pp. 2-18, Karlinsky was the first to discuss Nabokov's allusions to *Demon* and to those paintings by Vrubel of Lermontov's demon. Also see Proffer, "*Ada* as Wonderland," p. 428.

9. *Polnoe sobranie sochinenii* (Moscow-Leningrad: Gosizdat, 1947), II, xi, p. 161.

10. On Antiterra, Van tells us, "appeals to 'divine law' " have long ago been replaced "by common sense and popular science." In this context, incest is simply regarded as an "interference with the continuity of human evolution" (p. 133). Moral and religious restraints have evidently withered away under more powerful forces operating on Demonia. Quaint rituals still exist, but merely as remnants of some bygone system of belief, now defunct. For example, Lucette tells Van that his aerogram to Ada at Ardis Hall will not reach her as soon as he hopes; it will be carried by messenger on horse, "because on Sundays you could not use motorcycles, old local law, *l'ivresse de la vitesse, conceptions dominicales*" (p. 386).

11. "Moi rai, moi ad v tvoikh ochakh." *Demon*, II, x, p. 154.

12. In the mental hospital where tormented Aqua Veen is confined, the "most hateful" of her doctors is a connoisseur of love poetry—a "Cavalcanti quoter." Even the tap water in Aqua's room is full of "infernal ardor," singing like the "fluid and *flou* Italian verse" quoted by the hateful doctor. The dynamic source of energy on Antiterra is water, and in her madness Aqua associates the "hot torrent" of water flowing from the tap with the "infernal ardor" that courses through the demonic Veens and animates their relentless pursuit of lovely nymphs (pp. 23-24).

13. Nabokov's "Sovereign Society of Solicitous Republics" parodies the U.S.S.R.'s initials in Russian: S.S.S.R., standing for the *Soiuz Sovetskikh Sotsialisticheskikh Respublikh*.

14. Interview by James Mossman, p. 143, italics added.

15. Nabokov states that his "conception of the texture of time somewhat resembles its image in Part Four of *Ada*. The present is only the top of the past, and the future does not exist." Interview by Paul Sufrin, *Swiss Broadcast*, 8 September 1971; rpt. in *Strong Opinions*, p. 184.

VIII

On the Dark Side of Aesthetic Bliss: Nabokov's Humanism

1. *Laughter in the Dark*, trans. Vladimir Nabokov (1938; rpt. Norfolk, Conn.: New Directions, 1960), p. 143. All subsequent references to this edition will appear in the text.

2. See chapter 3, n. 4.

3. *The Metaphysical Foundations of Morals* (1785), trans. and ed. Carl J. Friedrich, in *The Philosophy of Kant: Immanuel Kant's Moral and Political Writings* (New York: Random House, 1949), pp. 176-177.

4. Possessing a steadier moral sense and a kinder heart, Nabokov's own poet, John Shade, would undoubtedly receive Humbert's glorification of the poet's morality with wry skepticism. Expressing a view similar to Humbert's, Shade's neighbor Kinbote assures him, "A poet's purified truth can cause no pain, no offense." "Sure, sure," the poet blandly counters. "One can harness words like performing fleas and make them drive other fleas. Oh, sure" (*Pale Fire*, p. 214). Shade's "performing fleas" recall Nabokov's own reference to his "galley slaves." Shade, like his author, understands that the artist strives for absolute mastery of his medium. His struggle to dominate, and subdue, both words and characters requires an effort of will that hardly suggests selfless devotion, or sanctity.

5. "In art, an individual style is essentially as futile and as organic as a fata morgana," said Nabokov in an interview by Allene Talmey, *Vogue*, December issue; rpt. in *Strong Opinions*, p. 153.

6. Interview by Herbert Gold, p. 94.

7. Interview by Kurt Hoffman, *Bayerischer Rundfunk*, October 1971; rpt. in *Strong Opinions*, p. 193.

Index

Index

Grayson, Jane, 174n2, 178n4, 186n6
Green, Martin, 107

Hardy, Barbara, 176n8
Harvey, W. J., 176n8
Hodgart, Matthew, 191n5
Howe, Irving, 91-93
Hughes, Daniel, 185n4
Hughes, Robert P., 182n8
Hyman, Stanley, 88

James, Henry, 122-124, 125, 128, 129, 132; *The Portrait of a Lady*, 126-127
Joyce, James, 179-180n17; *Ulysses*, 9, 10

Kant, Immanuel, 163
Karlinsky, Simon, 143, 174n2, 182n14, 191n8
Kenner, Hugh, 8, 190n2
Kermode, Frank, 88, 121, 173n2, 184n9
Khodasevich, Vladislav, 41, 175n4, 184-185n4

Leavis, F. R.: *The Great Tradition*, 189n6
Lenin, Nikolay, 179-180n17
Lermontov, Mikhail: *Demon*, 143, 148
Locke, John, 121

McCarthy, Mary, 16, 17, 32, 55, 120-121, 125, 188n18
Mandelstam, Nadezhda: *Hope Against Hope*, 85-86
Mandelstam, Osip, 85-86

Meredith, George, 122
Milton, John: *Paradise Lost*, 142-143
Murdoch, Iris, 175-176n8

Nabokov, Vera (Mrs. Vladimir), 191n5
Nabokov, Vladimir:
  Ada, 132-157, 158, 159, 169, 171, 190nn2, 3, 190-191n4, 191n5, 192nn10, 12, 15
  Bend Sinister, 6-7, 44, 49, 50, 51, 68-71, 72-85, 86-89, 90-91, 92, 93-96, 99, 103, 105-106, 178n8, 183n7, 183-184n9
  Despair, 3, 98-105, 106, 116, 184-185n4; *Otchaianie* (original Russian version), 104-105, 185n5, 185-186n6
  Invitation to a Beheading, 34, 44, 49, 50, 51, 52, 54, 55-67, 68, 69, 70, 71-72, 89-90, 95, 183n3, 186nn7, 10
  King, Queen, Knave, 14-15, 16, 17-22, 23-24, 26-31, 32-48, 71, 103, 106, 139, 163-164, 178n4, 179nn11, 12, 180-181n23
  Laughter in the Dark, 159-162, 163, 164, 165, 169, 171; *Kamera obskura* (original Russian version), 159
  Lolita, 3, 8, 9, 10, 98, 106-110, 130, 148-149, 155, 164-168, 169-170, 171,

196

Index

187n13, 190n3

Mashen'ka (Mary), 14, 15

Nikolai Gogol, 183n3

Pale Fire, 37, 44-45, 98, 110-118, 168, 187n15, 187-188n16, 188n18, 193n4

Pnin, 8

The Real Life of Sebastian Knight, 120, 130

Speak, Memory, 6-7, 52-53

Oates, Joyce Carol, 174n2

Praz, Mario: *The Romantic Agony*, 142-143, 191n7

Price, Martin, 176n8, 177n18

Proffer, Carl, 178n4, 180n20, 186n6, 190n1, 191n8

Pushkin, Alexander, 10; *Eugene Onegin*, 9, 10; *The Shot*, 185n5

Richardson, Samuel: *Pamela*, 127-128

Rosenfield, Claire, 185n4

Shakespeare, William, 6, 7; *Othello*, 100

Shklovsky, Viktor: "Art as Device," 24-25, 53

Solzhenitsyn, Alexander: *The Gulag Archipelago*, 65-66, 86, 182n14

Stalin, Joseph, 65-66, 85

Stegner, Page, 174n2, 187n15

Sterne, Laurence: *Tristram Shandy*, 88, 124-125, 184n9

Tillyard, E. W. 142

Tolstoy, Leo, 16, 24-25, 29; *War and Peace*, 32, 53-54

Toynbee, Philip, 173-174n2

Trilling, Diana, 77-78, 83

Van Ghent, Dorothy, 126-127

Vrubel, M. A., 191n8

Watt, Ian: *The Rise of the Novel*, 121-122, 125, 127-129

Woolf, Virginia, 176n8

Wordsworth, William, 43

Zola, Emile, 10